# the WITCH of the WOODS

### SPELLS, CHARMS, DIVINATION, REMEDIES, AND FOLKLORE

Written and illustrated by

## KILEY MANN

CICO BOOKS

LONDON NEW YORK

Published in 2022 by CICO Books
An imprint of Ryland Peters & Small Ltd

20–21 Jockey's Fields          341 E 116th St
London WC1R 4BW               New York, NY 10029

www.rylandpeters.com

10 9 8 7 6 5 4 3 2 1

Note: Please use caution when foraging or performing any of the rites
and rituals in this book. Do not touch any plants, fungi, or herbs you
are unsure about, and obey all applicable laws within your jurisdiction.
The publisher and author cannot accept any responsibility for loss or
damage arising from use of this book.

A CIP catalog record for this book is available from the
Library of Congress and the British Library.

ISBN: 978-180065-169-2
Printed in China

Commissioning editor: Carmel Edmonds
Editorial consultant: Cindy Richards
Editor: Slav Todorov
Designer: Allan Somerville
Art director: Sally Powell
Creative director: Leslie Harrington
Head of production: Patricia Harrington

# Contents

# Down the lonesome path

I HAVE SPENT MOST OF MY LIFE IN SOLITUDE, OR WISHING TO RETURN
TO IT. THIS SOLITUDE HAS DEFINED WHO I AM, WALKING ME DOWN THE
LONESOME PATH, ENDLESSLY GUIDING ME. I'VE FOUND THAT IN
SOLITUDE, THERE IS MUCH TO LEARN; FROM THE SOLITUDE ITSELF,
MOSTLY ABOUT OURSELVES.

I go to the woods often, without anything but myself. When I am alone, I become the woods. What happens on those paths is sacred and only known by a few. The lone soul I take into the woods to discover the world's secrets is my departed brother. His spirit dances among the pines and talks to the flowers. The trees do not mind him; as high as his spirit is, they always love a child at heart. Most of all, he listens to what the land wants to say. These lands are walked, but seldom noticed. However, he takes every step with curiosity, waiting to see what the world has to tell him. He has taught me that in this land there are souls waiting to teach us, if we will only listen to the winds.

The unique lesson the wind teaches us is that there is no one right way to follow the ways of the land. Depending on what region your family is from, the wind will speak differently to you and you will practice accordingly. The winds of the north teach very differently to the winds of the south; however, they are

both simply winds. The similarities we find in the folk magic practices of different regions are much greater than the differences, as the wind is what unites us all.

For the longest time the old folk, or those living in farming communities throughout the old forests of northern Michigan, were rightfully afraid of the monsters that lurked up in the hills and the people who knew how to tame them. This fear didn't go away, despite what people in town might say. There's still a suspicion about the wildness of the woods and what magic might lie hidden in the trees. Herein lies our connection to what it means to be a folk worker: A deep connection to the land that we walk and the land we must use all eyes to view. This connection crosses all cultural and personal boundaries. In this way, we as a younger generation can embrace the strength and wisdom of the past while understanding that all traditions must evolve.

The works and the ways in this book are from the winds of the North Midwestern woods, both old and new. Their roots are true and deep in these forests. This book is my attempt at piecing together years of whipping gales and slow breezes. Take what you will, as we are bound to miss some lessons here and there. This work is what I know, but there is always more to the unknown than we recognize. This practice is not one that falls under a label, it is not religion and it is not a spirituality. It is simply what it is. It's very much disappearing—some would say dying, but I choose to say changing.

## Northern magic

The folklore and magic of the north is specific to this region of the Midwestern area: We're not so much about long ago and far away as we are about this place and what's going on here and now. When you

*Folklore depicts our bare fears and anxieties, while at the same time, in full counterpoint, reveals our visions and hopes.*

> High summer comes with
> an abundance of long days
> of roaming the fields.

live in a place where the climate can kill you, you learn to pay close attention to your surroundings and the effects of the simple happenings around us.

Folklore is a small area of research in the humanities, and it is fairly unique in every country or region. At the same time no branch of study, academic or popular, penetrates as deeply into our intuitive life or mirrors its contemplative self as clearly as folklore. Folklore depicts our bare fears and anxieties, while at the same time, in full counterpoint, revealing our visions and hopes.

It is the way of this land that shapes us and connects our livelihoods to those around us. Folk magic, in itself, is a method of survival using the ways of the land. There are still rural areas holding pockets of some old folkways, but for the most part, as with many other American folk traditions, most of this knowledge, which at one time would have been so vital to survival and livelihood, is now limited to

such "practice." When the topics of survival and livelihood arise, we must pay our respects to marginalized peoples where these practices took root. Because these traditions came about as a result of from persecution, they became deeply integrated into the old ways of life. If we begin to practice any form of folk magic while dismissing its roots, or even simply being unaware of them, this is simply disrespectful to time-honored communities.

Certain forms of magic are initiatory, closed, or require some sort of ancestral connection—for example, Judaism or Vodou. Such practices are often referred to as "closed" in the magic community. When we step into the world of folk magic, it is of the utmost importance not to overstep boundaries into closed practices where we do not belong. Many folk magical practices were created as a byproduct of cultural mingling across many groups of people, so researching the roots behind the practices you

# Map of home

choose to engage in is crucial to deeper understanding and respectful execution. There are, in fact, many spells and practices prevalent in folk magic that are exclusive to such closed practices.

Twenty-first century witchcraft on a large scale is deeply rooted in and influenced by Wicca and New Age concepts, which are themselves heavily, heavily influenced by many closed practices. Personal discernment is key to understanding the nuances that come with closed and open practices. Research, interaction with firsthand sources, and an open mind are absolutely necessary.

As mentioned before, much of folk magic originated from the persecution of marginalized groups. The reason why it is important to research before you practice is simply out of respect for the groups who began these practices. By practicing these closed practices (knowingly or unknowingly) it is inherently disrespectful toward the culture, religion, or group that they originated from, while also de-sanctifying an otherwise very important aspect of someone's being.

## The old ways

The huge majority of the people from closed practice were historically forced to abandon their beliefs or hide them, or forced to follow a foreign religion imposed by colonialist authorities. Their beliefs survived. We need to know this and grow from this. What we can personally do is pay attention to and amplify the voices of witches of closed practices, and think about how we can respect these practices. The first step is educating yourself on the countless different types of closed practices. Since many of these practices relied on the oral repetition of stories and spells passed down through generations, there is often not much recorded or academic material on the subject.

There are still those in the region who are working hard to preserve what little material is still out there, and to educate others about these folkways before they're lost forever. I've been a part of this struggle for years now, collecting my own folk material, and traditional working methods of healing into my own practice. There is no singular word for what the world has to teach us. Some might call it folk magic —I call it the way of the woods.

These are the charms of my family, and I will teach you these ways if you promise to uphold their roots. This is my offering to these woods, to the history of the lakes, and the future of the lessons of the wind.

These lands all have lessons to teach us, unique in their own characteristics and being. You must walk the land to know it. You cannot know her if you do not let your feet touch the ground and wander aimlessly as you please. These lessons are taught directly through the land itself. Come, as we go barefoot wandering through the lands of the north.

# Part One

# THE
# FOLKLORE

# CHAPTER ONE

# Barefoot wandering

## THE NORTH

### Seasons of the north

### The swamp

### The forest

### The lake

# The north

THE LAND WHERE I BEGAN TO LEARN OF THE WINDS IS IN A RURAL NORTHERN AMERICAN TOWN. THE PEOPLE HERE CARE LITTLE FOR THESE STORIES AND TALES, LEAVING THE LAND UNTOUCHED. TERRAIN HELPS SHAPE AND SHIFT THE MINDSETS OF THESE PEOPLE. TO UNDERSTAND THE STRANGE WAY OF THE CRAFT YOU HAVE TO UNDERSTAND THE WAY THE LAND LIVES.

For me, these beckoning old woods, valleys of graveyards, and winding hilltop trails were the fertile grounds for superstitions and beliefs to grow. The chilling bobcat shrieks and legends of forest dwellers were enough to temper me with a careful hand, not to tempt fate. These woods are enchanting; their darkness in nature just as much so.

The northern lands of the Midwest are ever-changing, particularly due to the unpredictable weather of this area. Others say that the wooded hills are the backs of trolls, curled up in resting sleep. These trolls move ever so slowly, so we will only notice the land has moved once the years have flown by. In some parts of the forest, the brush is as dense and thick as the skies of winter. Sometimes moss covers the forest floor. Small ravines, grassy fields, and sand dunes appear on the landscape as well. The seasons change rapidly and bring with them fresh sights, sounds, and experiences.

# SEASONS OF THE NORTH

The ravines and streams run solely through the woods, with rocky banks and bottoms. If you look close enough, you can find a lone sparkling lump of quartz. We walk these woods with nothing but the bare bottoms of our feet: As my mom always said, that's the easiest way to get to know the land. Scarce boulders older than the wood itself are scattered around the forests. These stones grow mossy and weathered from the rains of the spring and autumn.

The northern region has a strange pattern of climatic conditions. Well, it isn't a pattern at all. The weather we experience is sporadic, bringing feet of snow and storms of hail. The lake is the bringer of such conditions, as she can never really make up her mind on the weather. The old folk despised this uncertainty, and we still haven't quite figured out how the northern weather lake system works to this day. However, there's one thing you can count on— a heavy winter.

As summer takes her leave for sleep, we are left chilled by the winter gales. The leaves have long been brown, and now we will be surrounded by white-covered land for long months to come. Winter often consumes half the seasons, calling for year-round preparations and gathering of resources. Most animals hibernate. However, some brave the winter— you can often find a lone deer, coyote, or turkey rummaging the woodland grounds. The wind is whipping, and the temperature often drops below zero. When it becomes this cold, we call it "soul chilling." In winter everything lies dormant in the silent earth; it is a sacred time of rest and reflection before the awakening and the slow build toward brighter days. Spirits run high this time of year, making their presence felt in the mortal world on the winter solstice.

We often have false springs following winter, where we think it'll be the last frost and the weather will finally become warm. Then comes the next week and we'll be knee-deep in snow again. These forests protect us from the unpredictable conditions that the lake creates, which is why so many folks live out in the boonies. Oftentimes, the daffodils will sprout too early, only to be buried by a final snow. You never really know when to sow your seeds here.

Sooner than the blink of an eye, the liminal period of muddied snow and gray skies turns to budding leaves and leek soup. This time of the year we often receive something called trillium snow. These blessed white flowers litter the forest floor, making it look like winter. The trilliums are sacred and mustn't be disturbed. If you dare pluck a trillium, it'll bring on an early winter come autumn. Then the morels start to grow.

> *High summer comes with an abundance of long days of roaming the fields.*

Morels mark the beginning of summer in the following weeks. For now, it is still a cool, wet spring, just when the mayapples spread their umbrellas and apple blossoms hang heavy on the trees in town. Morels are notoriously wise, rumored to hold the secrets of all life. They teach patience and caution; as a morel won't come up if the ground is too dry, or conditions are otherwise unfavorable. The next town over from my own has a morel mushroom festival, all to celebrate the greatness of this singular fungus.

You can always tell when the morels have finished growing by the blooms on the blackberry bushes. Once the blackberry buds start to flower, it is the end of morel-foraging season. The trees still have a little more to grow, as it's only the middle of May. The weather is beginning to warm up and the lady of the lake begins to calm. The hills are awake and the animals are again abundant—vultures looking for a hard-earned meal, tadpoles swimming in pools, and foxes roaming where they ought not to.

High summer comes with an abundance of long days of roaming the fields. This time of year I am found entranced in the summer heat, finally taking a break from my labors. The summer solstice is a time to celebrate the height of the season, and to honor and welcome that energy into our life. After the longest day passes and the fireflies begin to fade, late summer is heralded by fields of mullein and abundant oyster mushrooms. However, the height of the heat is tempered by the dog days—the season when misfortunes are said to run highest.

After the dog days have passed, we arrive at the final weeding of the gardens and harvesting of herbs. The leaves turn a variety of autumn shades, littering the sky, and finally the ground. The lands become ablaze with the urgent energy of animals searching for their winter meals. The dirt is finally turned as the first frost comes along. The winds bring the witch of November and the cycle begins again.

# A wild foraging calendar

### EARLY SPRING—SPRING

*Burdock root, dandelion root, garlic, mustard, maple sap, wild cherry bark, witch hazel bark, white willow bark, chickweed, nettle leaf, birch sap, pussy willow, apple blossoms, horsetail leaf flower, ground ivy leaf, wild lettuce tops, rose petals*

### EARLY SUMMER—SUMMER

*Cleavers, herbs, raspberry, mullein leaf, lemon balm leaf, chamomile flower, mints, yarrow leaf and flower, catnip, coltsfoot, oat flower tops, dandelion flower and straws, garden sage, echinacea flower, California poppy, linden leaf flower, wormwood leaf, hawthorn leaf and flower, St. John's flower, beebalm flower*

### FALL—LATE FALL

*Elderberry, fever fern leaf, yarrow leaf and flower, sumac, goldenrod flowering tops, wild yew root, blue vervain, mugwort leaf and flower, calendula flowers, angelica tree root, mullein flower, valerian root, wort licorice, lavender leaf and flower, rose hips*

### WINTER

*Juniper berries, marshmallow root, balsam, pine needles, chicory root, gravel root, ashwagandha root, bird berry, hemlock, white pine, apple wool, Queen Anne's lace seed, juniper, cedar wood, bearberry*

# THE SWAMP

The land will always inform your practice; the northern swamps inform mine. The land is where you learn to grow, and in turn we care for the land to ensure this growth. Swamps have the ability to create life and preserve death in subtle ways right before our eyes. Being a place of great power, the swamp's energy can be used for whatever you please (with her permission, of course). Even people lacking intuitive senses can feel the energy of a swamp. No other place offers such a feeling of heavy suffocation. Often people are afraid of wetlands and what they hold inside, refusing to set foot due to its inexplicable, mystic energy.

I am drawn to the swamp's practicality, and in particular to the duality she represents. The swamp in my backyard is alluring; however, the power she possesses is unbearable. I have learned that the discomfort she causes is merely a result of her magnitude. The more I embrace the swamp, the more I find myself embracing the darker forms in life. There is a wholeness to the swamp, and we can exist in wholeness. After all, the nature of the swamp itself exhibits the boundary betwen life and death.

The swamp I grew up by was a haven for all things beautiful. Mother Nature flourished on this land, creating a powerful area to call home. I walked down to the swamp whenever I needed to recollect myself, release anger, or simply to talk. I became close friends with the swamp over the years, learning the ins and outs of her ways. Whenever she had something particularly important to tell me, she would send geese into our yard. There was a time where we even found a pair of goslings on our porch. The swamp is particularly bold in her ways.

Swamps, bogs, marshes, and fens are havens for poisonous things, flora, and fauna alike. Spirits are drawn to these areas—swamps hold the necessary qualities of life and death that sustain their existence in the physical realm. Naturally, the veil is thin in such wetlands. I've found that to walk the ground of the swamp, you absolutely must please the spirits of the swamp. First you must know what they desire.

*If you take more than you require, the spirits and the lady will be angered by your greed.*

# Swamp weeds

### SKULLCAP

*A plant of faithfulness and loyalty, skullcap is used to keep peace and reduce stress. It also can be used to break charms. Skullcap is excellent for banishing unwanted visitors.*

### RED DOGWOOD

*The dogwood is a tree of resurrection and changing perceptions. They signal caution as well as trusting their intuition and reflections.*

### FERN

*Ferns are plants of death and rebirth. They can be used for vitality and healing as well as contacting spirits. Use a fern when you need help with extreme growth and change.*

### SWAMP MARIGOLD

*Marigold is a plant of death and happiness at the same time. It is used to promote legal matters as well as positivity, happiness, and stability.*

### JOE PYE WEED

*Often used for love and respect, this weed is frequently carried for good luck. It can be used to give warnings and keep up wards and protections in the home.*

### SWAMP NETTLE

*Nettle is a motherly plant, healing and stinging at the same time. Use nettle to heal a broken heart. It can be used for love.*

### MINT

*Mint is used for intuition, change, as well as getting a fresh start.*

### CATTAIL

*The cattail is used for fertility, love, lust and sexual tendencies.*

Luckily, most of the time it is something that will bring life.

The swamp itself is the presiding spirit of all marshes and fens. She is the giving force for all that exists within her territory. The spirits that reside there are a menagerie of adopted families. Never try to banish a spirit from a swamp, even if it's in your backyard, as the swamp is their home and we are merely visitors. Never defile the swamp or take from her without permission. If you take more than you require, the spirits and the lady will be angered by your greed. The spirits of the swamp are protective of their resources, as it is what gives them life. Taking part of the swamp without the approval of the lady is a surefire way not to be welcomed back.

Swamp spirits are mischievous in nature, never causing immediate or severe harm. Instead, when they are angered, they prefer to trick us in material and psychological ways. Perhaps you may not be able to find your way out of the swamp, or might even develop an inexplicable fear of entering the swamp grounds, preventing you from safely entering without worry ever again. Instead of harming you, the spirits will choose to protect themselves and their home by deterring you. To remain in good standing with the swamp and her spirits, listen to what they have to say.

The swamp herself is a powerful witch, showing herself only to those who choose to swim in her murky waters. She can often be found in her more obvious form, the sandhill crane. When you see a crane on the swampland, it is the witch making sure we are aware of the swamp's existence, despite her solemn appearances.

Her extreme sacred energy, combined with the thinning of the veil, makes the swamp an ideal place for workings of all sorts. However, the swamp demands a certain respect in return for her fruits. I often leave offerings on her lily pads, such as herbs from my garden, eggshells and such. You must be mindful of the swamp and everything that resides within it. Recognize her danger, but also appreciate her beauty, biodiversity, and bountifulness. She will provide for us, that is, if we respect her potency. The swamp has the capacity to preserve within her deepest, darkest depths. She has the energy to destroy those who cross her. Most importantly, she has the energy to create, no matter what she is given.

> *The swamp herself is a powerful witch, showing herself only to those who choose to swim in her murky waters.*

# THE FOREST

The forest is the son of the swamp, sharing her ability to promote and sustain life. He fathers the creatures of the woods and tends to the flora and fungi. If you have ever stumbled upon a stick hut, you have seen the home of the man of the forest. He was once human, but in his earlier days he fell in love with an old cedar tree. The cedar tree loved him equally, and made him an offer that if he remained in the forest forever, he could stay with her. And so, he stayed. He now wanders the forests of the north, half human, half tree. When he is alone, he works freely, gathering food and creating paths and trails. However, once he hears the footsteps of a lone wanderer, you will have trouble identifying him as he turns into whatever tree he pleases.

The energy of the forest is primeval. The murmuring pines and hemlocks bearded with moss stand like druids who wait to speak their prophecies. He seeks to have you understand his ways, so that you can know him completely. He is wise, as he holds the knowledge of everything he grows. He hears the secrets of those who walk his paths. However, he is trustworthy, providing a place of refuge for all.

I grew up with the woods of my hometown, watching the trees twist and mangle around the age-old barbed wire fence. I've found the knowledge of the woods is deeply hidden, and that you must gain the trust of the forest to benefit from its wisdom. Beware of looking too deep, as you might peer past the darkness.

> *There are secrets in these woods that are not of man. Walk his trails long enough and you will start to lose your sense of self.*

The dark side of the forest is not as subtle as that of the swamp, who slowly absorbs you into her muddy waters. The forest can instill fear the moment you disregard his being. His creatures can be menacing, having no regard for human life. The man of the woods prefers his time alone at night, so he can commune with his creatures and the cedar trees. Lest you enter the woods at night and disturb his peace, he will make sure you solemnly enter again.

The privacy of the forest must be respected, for he might send his most ferocious beast to add your soul to his collection. There are secrets in these woods that are not of man. Walk his trails long enough and you will start to lose your sense of self. The backwoods are here to teach us that not everything is meant to be known, and that there is something to be learned from the act of minding your own business.

# THE LAKE

And the lake, the beloved daughter of the swamp, is the healing force within us all. Her water is enchanting and restorative. The energy she holds is infinite, constantly creating anew with every wave on the shore. There is a lot to learn from the lake: How to heal, how to love, and how to cleanse our soul. Lake water is extremely refreshing, being able to wash away the most stubborn energies. She is purifying in nature, cleansing our soul and mind.

The lake has a welcoming nature, but at a cost. She demands you hold her in high regard, lest she wash you into her depths. She appears with her kindly demeanor to visitors, beckoning them in. True friends of the lake know never to enter her waters without giving a gift in her honor. To bathe in her is to absorb her energy. We must give in return for what we take.

Swimming in her summer morning water is almost a ritual of sorts. You almost never enter the lake without skipping a stone first. This is a way of giving her a simple "hello" and warning that you are about to enter her waters. The smart thing to do is to skip three stones before you even dip your toes in the lake. One stone means "hello," the second means "I'm coming in," and the third stone is always a "thank you."

Although the lake is cleansing, she isn't exactly the best source of stable energy. She is ever-changing and can never make up her mind. Her waters are ideal for bringing on new beginnings and adapting to change. The lake is versatile and will never sit still. This constant roll of tides within her depths makes her an excellent source for rebirthing the self.

The lady of the lake is a giver and a taker, notorious for her November storms and ability to take the lives of men with the power of her waves. She looks as powerful as she is, although I have only seen her once. She wears a dress destroyed by whipping wind, with great antlers that grow from her long, dark hair. If you look deep enough into her gown, you can see how her history crashes with her waves.

If you walk far enough into the woods, you'll see the stream that runs warm, the paranormal, and the witchcraft that whispers on foggy mornings. Swim deep enough into the waters and you feel the eerie touch of natural forces. Let's turn now to the creatures of these woods: The dwelling fae, the unseen troll knocking at the door, and the strange in-betweens.

*Swim deep enough into the waters and you feel the eerie touch of natural forces.*

# CHAPTER TWO

# Folks on the hill

## MYSTERIOUS TALES

### Mushrooms

### Folklore

# Mysterious tales

THE STORIES FOUND IN THESE WOODS ARE WHERE I LEARNED MY CRAFT: HOW TO HEAL, PRECAUTIONS AGAINST MISFORTUNE, AND THE SPIRITS OF THE LAND. THERE ARE TALES OF CREATURES THAT LIVE IN THE PINES, OLD WOMEN OF THE SWAMPS, AND MUSHROOMS CREATED FROM THE FLESH OF GOD HIMSELF. WE'LL START WITH THE LATTER.

## MUSHROOMS

I was told that when God created flora, fauna, and all things living, he created mushrooms as a trace of his own divinity on earth. God took flesh from his body and created the first fungi, which had the ability to spread infinitely. Fungi make worlds, and they can also unmake them. They are what we used to be, what we could be, and what we eventually will be. Mushrooms carry unlimited divine information and God-given intimate secrets within their spores.

Mushroom hunting was a sacred activity, and I was taught to respect the mushrooms that grew in our forest as such. When we set out into the woods after a fresh rain, my mom would walk with me and teach me about the trees and the spirits they held within. We always had to watch our step, for if we accidentally trod on a mushroom we were fated to find none that

day, so had to return home. Picking the mushroom itself was its own rite and ritual; we made sure to harvest the fungi correctly to promote continued growth. Caring for the forest included harvesting her mushrooms, except the poisonous ones.

I was always told the fae inhabited any poisonous mushroom, so I was not to touch or disturb them. My parents allowed these mushrooms to grow and flourish in our yard, and I was always entranced by their mysticism. I never bothered these mushrooms, being afraid that the fae would mess with me or my little brother, causing us to get lost on the way home, or make important objects to go suddenly missing. However, as I found out later in my practice, they are incredibly useful in many types of spellwork.

> *There is mysticism and knowledge hidden within our everyday lives. It shows the knowledge passed down from our ancestors.*

My mother was always taking the necessary precautions to keep us safe as we explored the woods. Bells were hung around the boundaries of our house, along with wind chimes. When these bells rang, the fae were trying to push past her warded boundaries. Whenever we left her sight, she would put almonds in our pockets to deter any spirits. As we returned home, we had to eat the almonds before entering the house.

While I was taught that the fae were dangerous at times, they preferred mischief over peril. My mother respected their existence and the places they resided. My dad, on the other hand, dealt with the consequences of disrespecting the fae for years. The only conflict we had was their tendency to favor our garden. My mother and I would gather supplies and make fairy houses out of sticks so that they would happily move from the garden into their new homes. It always worked.

## FOLKLORE

You may be wondering how exactly these folk tales relate to the craft. These stories define the mindset of our everyday interactions. Even the smallest of creatures demands respect and the most ferocious-looking beasts can provide knowledge. Not all is as it seems. There is mysticism and knowledge hidden within our everyday lives. It shows the knowledge passed down from our ancestors and the ancient wisdom we can gain from their tales.

The stories that are presented to us are the mother and grandmother of the craft. They teach us to be kind and careful, but stoical and strong. They teach us, most importantly, to mind our own most of the time, and act otherwise if we would like to see what happens. Here are some examples of the creatures and spirits of folklore that I grew up with:

# TROLLS

Trolls can survive extreme weather conditions and therefore tend to settle as far as possible from human civilization. They are most common in the woods, where they sleep for years on end, and are often mistaken for hills. Trees grow abundantly on the trolls' backs, as they are not bothered by the roots digging into their skin. When the hill trolls awaken, they make their way to the lakes where they can live peacefully underwater without drawing attention. Smaller trolls are more likely to live near swamps where they can burrow and create a home deep in the mud. When a swamp troll is submerged, the only visible parts of his body are usually the hump and top of his head, which look like partially water-covered rocks; the creature's long hair looks like grass. They are more common in the far north, where it is dark for months at a time.

Trolls are very large, carnivorous amphibians with voracious appetites. Many sport large, hooked noses, and hair covered in water plants; others are sheltered in trees and moss. They have long, drooping ears to prevent water entering their ear canals, and overly large hands and feet for swimming. They are extremely old, and covered in wrinkles and moles. In fact, I have never heard of the death or birth of a troll; they might as well be immortal.

It would be unwise to try to befriend a troll, as they do not understand the concept of companionship. Although trolls are known for their kidnapping tendencies, this isn't for the company. It's to make sure they have something for dinner. They have no heart in their body, causing a lack of empathy and basic emotional understanding. But beware: Trolls are particularly cunning with their words if you happen to find yourself among them.

To escape a troll, you must trick them. It's never a matter of personal strength, as trolls can be the size of mountains. Tales tell us that humans are best advised to avoid them, but if one must confront them, be persistent. The only things that repel trolls are: Your own intellect, a bag of teeth, and a lightning storm. Be careful next time you walk up a hill.

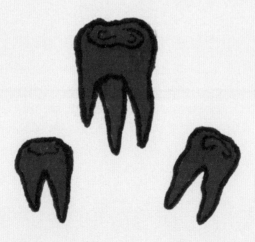

## TOADS AND FROGS

Toads have long been associated with magic, as familiars, and as a source of energy in folk healing. These amphibious critters are known for a variety of magical properties, from their ability to help predict the weather to bringing good luck.

It is believed in these woods that if you hear a frog croaking exactly at midnight, it means rain is on the way. On the other hand, if you hear a frog croak at noon, it will be clear through the night. Having a toad approach your doorstep is considered good luck, and a harbinger of new opportunity. To kill a toad or frog will bring instant misfortune upon the toad-killer and their family, and their families' for generations to come.

That being said, toads are extremely valuable creatures, with the ability to both curse and bless. For those taking up residence in a new property, there is a certain woodland ritual employing the toad that will make a new home protected and secure. A fine, lumpy toad is to be carried to the front door of the property, and solemnly brought through the house and out of the rear door. Here, in the garden of the property, the creature is set free to dwell and care is taken to ensure that its needs are met and comforts provided for. The presence of the lumpy toad will bestow blessings of good fortune upon the property and its inhabitants, as well as ensuring a fruitful garden and harvests to come.

> *Toads are extremely valuable creatures, with the ability to both curse and bless.*

## WILL-O'-THE-WISPS

Will-o'-the-wisps are strange beings, and will typically appear in groups. Keep your eyes out for a bunch of flickering lights where lights ought not to be. Often found near swamps or ponds, or floating over fields, they have a knack for luring humans into the woods at night. They purposefully lure in inquisitive people or children who are likely to follow them out of curiosity. In certain situations, if you ever catch yourself following a wisp, a bribe can be made. But, never break your promise to a wisp.

Once a man who had lost his way offered two silver coins if the wisp would lead him home. The wisp agreed, and finally they arrived at the man's house. He thanked his guide—but instead of the promised payment, he gave the wisp only a small copper coin. As the man opened his front door and took a step forward, he stepped deep into a murky swamp. As he looked around, he realized he was no longer at his front door, but somewhere very, very far away.

If you are looking to get lost, the wisp can show you the ways to certain herbs, magical surroundings, and tools. I've heard of wisps leading a curious person out to the woods, only to reward him with fields of wildflowers and a beautiful stream. Other times, you will find yourself knee-deep in the mud, far away from the safety of your loving home.

> *Familiars have been known to appear in the guise of or inhabit animals, but the animal itself is a vessel, not the familiar itself.*

## FAMILIARS

Familiars are a category of animistic spirits, particularly those with whom you have a magical bond. These spirits attend their chosen individual even after death. Such bonds can only be found naturally, not purchased or purposefully sought out. If it aligns with your path, your familiar will find you when the time is right. Your paths are likely to cross unexpectedly. You'll feel the soul connection immediately and possess an inherent understanding of one another. They may enhance your energy during magical work and be eager to get involved. You may seem able to communicate with them telepathically as well. This is not a definitive list of criteria to determine if your pet is a familiar, merely some commonly recognized traits. More often than not, your pet isn't a familiar, and assigning them as such can put them in a position of danger.

When a familiar spirit chooses to embody themselves in an animal, it's always for a particular reason. By doing so, it is able to exhibit the characteristics of that animal and seeks to teach or serve through these means. Even though the spirit may have a life of its own, it seeks to remain in close companionship to whoever it has chosen.

Familiars, to get this out of the way, are not animals. They are—and always will be—spirits. Familiars have been known to appear in the guise of or inhabit animals, but the animal itself is a vessel, not the familiar itself. Whether it is passed down through the family (or from mentor to student), or whether it is given to you by the universe itself, a familiar is not a servant—it's a partnership. They will not follow your every command and will retaliate if you treat them in this way. It is give and take on both sides.

# A familiar can be any animal, but these are by far the most common:

## CATS

*Cats are intuitive beings, graceful in nature and possessed of slyness. They often bring adaptability and longevity. Having a cat as a familiar means that they will often help with divinations and assists with moving in and out of the spirit realm. They assist in death and spiritual types of spells, and helps in protection and sensing energies.*

## SNAKES

*When a familiar appears as a snake, they aid in strengthening regeneration and the healing of the mind, body, and soul. On the other hand, banishing rites are also best aided by the familiar snake. They can also help us to see through the deception and lies of others, and in turn, speak our own truth.*

## BEES

*Bees are symbols of the family and the home, helping us build steady foundations for a community. A familiar can often take the form of a full hive of bees, each tiny creature carrying the energy of this familiar. Bees are very helpful in whatever you choose to do, especially in helping you to improve your work ethic.*

## RABBITS

*Familiars appear as rabbits when they wish to bring tenacity and playfulness into your life. They are symbols of fertility and creativity, often referred to as bringers of life. A rabbit familiar often gives us telltale signs when somebody is trying to affect our energy, as they are very alert beings.*

## SONGBIRDS

*As a familiar, songbirds in general can guide our lives toward perceptiveness, although each species has its own characteristics. Often aiding in astral work, having a bird as a familiar is generally helpful when exploring new areas of knowledge.*

## TOADS

*As mentioned previously, toads are particularly lucky. They are masters of prophecy in life, helping us to transform and grow into what we are meant to be. They represent fertility and wisdom, and in the familiar form, will often guide us in making prophecies and obtaining abundance.*

## CROWS

*Crows are highly perceptive beings, capable of recognizing faces and mimicking sounds. They are masters of deception and mischief, and the bringers of particular omens. When familiars appear as crows, they are renowned for their message-carrying abilities and their help in matters of communications.*

## GNOMES

Gnomes are of the friendly folk, but prefer to avoid human contact. Often, if you find a gnome wandering about, it will immediately burrow into the ground. However, these beings are particularly wise, and are often sought out for their words of wisdom. They prefer to live in the roots of old trees, often leaving gnome-sized doors at the base of old oaks or elms. Burrowing systems of tunnels through the ground, they are known protectors of roots in gardens. In appearance, they stand about six inches tall and mature rather quickly, appearing old even as infants.

Gnomes hold infinite knowledge about the forest and its flora, fauna, and fungi. They are excellent foragers, notoriously eating mushrooms, root vegetables, and bird eggs. They are extremely in tune with nature and often feel the emotions of the forest itself. Gentle in nature, they can frequently be seen riding the backs of small animals such as squirrels or rabbits. They are protectors of all life and like to ensure that every living creature remains unharmed. They are known to plant seeds wherever they go to ensure the growth of the forest.

Many people regard gnomes as rather unintelligent, owing to their size. Yet I most remember the gnomes I met in childhood for their eccentric sense of humor, inquisitiveness, and engineering prowess. Most gnomes are content to live simple lives, acquiring knowledge merely as a hobby. But others explored lost ruins, delved deep into the heart of the world, or undertook dangerous explorations in their unquenchable thirst for knowledge, leading more than a few to an untimely demise.

If you happen upon a gnome and wish to befriend him, offer him a stone—preferably one of value such as an agate or other gemstone. Instead of running in fear, he'll be compelled to add it to his collection. Offer him the stone, but only if you are allowed to wander the forest together.

# CHAPTER THREE

# Spill some wine

**ANCESTRAL WORK**

Honoring the dead

Offerings

Communication

Where the yew bushes grow

# Ancestral work

ANCESTRAL WORK IS A MOURNFUL THING, A FEELING OF BEING SWEPT
DOWNSTREAM IN A FAST-MOVING CURRENT OF LIVES THAT ENDED TOO
QUICKLY. IT'S A CLAMORING OF LONG-FORGOTTEN VOICES VYING FOR
ATTENTION, FOR CARE; AND THE UNTANGLING OF THOUSANDS TO
FOLLOW SO FEW. TO FIND KIN AND LISTEN TO THEIR SONGS AND STORIES,
TO SEEK THEM OUT AND ACCEPT THEM, IS TO ACCEPT THE UNRAVELING
OF HARD TRUTHS.

Many of my ancestors passed in their recent coming to America or as a result of trying to escape the homeland of the Jewish people and of the Slavic communities. While my ancestry is rooted in assimilation of many groups and peoples, they have one thing in common: They were strong enough to overcome the persecution and differences in culture.

Through ancestral work, your ancestors can become your biggest supporters and protectors. A lot of people view this work as a trade: You make an offering and they'll grant a favor. I'm here to tell you that this is the furthest thing from the truth. In this line of work you'll meet ancestors who were very bad in life, who shine a light on the faults of your own blood. We mustn't ignore these ancestors as they are the ones who present us with the task of healing ourselves and those who follow us. To ignore the ancestors that exist within our lineage is to ignore the

crimes they perpetuated. I will not explain how to atone for what some of our ancestors have done, as that's up to you. You will benefit greatly from putting in the work to heal your lineage. However, in order to commune with these ancestors, you must have a relationship with them. That, I will teach you.

To understand our ancestors, we must understand death and its impact on us. Death is the source of most fear, creating stories, folklore, personifications, and metaphors in the wake of its creeping shadow. Most everybody thinks about death during their lifetime; however, few face it with broad shoulders and stern eyes. The shadow of death has had a great impact on those who choose to study the ways of the dead—or, in fact, anyone at all. I was taught never to focus on death, as it is more important to focus on the world to come.

Death is an inevitable phenomenon, yet is regarded with such anxiety. In essence, it is a continuation of life: A method of existence outside of bodily function. Just as grief is an extension of love, so death is an extension of life. Taking away the threat of eternal damnation or the reward of golden fields creates less fear around the matter. Death is, simply, as death is. While the thought of afterlife doesn't matter so much, making sure our ancestors are well comforted in the liminal space they exist within is central in my family's craft.

## HONORING THE DEAD

The love and honor we show our ancestors is instilled at a young age. We give them food. We never speak ill of the dead, or walk on their gravestones, and dismissing their presence is frowned upon. Many honor their ancestors without conscious awareness, such as hanging their pictures on the wall, or imagining them as a guardian angel. Some people make shrines, or have a small designated space to the spirit of that person. Many, including myself, create a space for all ancestors to commune and be honored. This not only creates a place for them in your home, but in your life too. You'll be reminded of them every time you walk by.

My own ancestral shrine is on a black bookshelf in the corner of my room. This shrine changes and adapts to where I go and what I do; it almost always looks different. Though I do not have many heirlooms of those that have passed, I keep items in memory of their spirit. I have my great grandfather's watch; a book of Hebrew hymns gifted to me from my childhood rabbi; antlers from family hunting trips; perfume and oils; a picture of my great-great grandfather Ole; and some yew branches and frankincense gum.

Some people follow certain rules in ancestor veneration, such as only honoring blood relatives, or always having an offering to hand. I believe you should honor whoever, and however, feels right. I honor my mom's best friend Jinx who passed away from cancer. She loved me from the moment she met me, so I consider her family, regardless of blood connection. Honoring the dead can just be about your ancestors, but you can add in a certain loved one as well.

As this book concerns my own family practices, I can offer you this: Pay attention to the daily stories, your dreams, and to your own behavior. The roots beneath it all will show themselves in time. Maybe they are lingering in your childhood memories, or maybe it's something you'd rather not speak of. Take it to the dead. They will know what to say.

# OFFERINGS

As far as offerings go, my mom taught me to always have a gift for the spirits. Even if they don't accept it, they'll appreciate the gesture. My mom's favorite offering for spirits is growing plants. She grows a flower bush or a houseplant and dedicates it to a certain person, making sure to care for it as it grows. When Jinx passed, her husband gifted my mom a weeping fig tree. Over the years, she's grown and nurtured it to be as strong-standing as Jinx was. My mom often says it carries a piece of her spirit.

For other offerings, I often leave family foods and desserts on my ancestor altar for them to enjoy. They'll let you know when they're done with them. A glass of water is always nice too; whiskey or wine for the elders on special occasions. I've found my ancestors particularly enjoy fresh yew branches, as they are often associated with crossing over to the other side. You'll need to learn your ancestors' tastes.

Talk to your relatives about them, and then talk to the spirits. When we listen to our ancestors, we learn lessons they have learned throughout the years.

It's also a common practice to dedicate a candle to your ancestor or a specific member of the dead. By devoting this object to them, you will be able to communicate with them through the flame or smoke. Offerings would then be left for the dead, often alongside lighted candles—so that the souls could find their way. People also tried to communicate with their ancestors through prayers, songs, and even trance-like states. It was believed that the dead are not fully gone, but can still answer us and wander our world to drink, eat, talk, and visit their beloved family.

To give more context on exactly how long an offering should be left out, I prefer to group my offering into five main groups: Permanent, temporary, perishable, acts of devotion, and burnt offerings.

> I've found my ancestors particularly enjoy fresh yew branches, as they are often associated with crossing over to the other side.

## Permanent offerings

Permanent offerings are most often left on my altar for extended periods of time, only to be removed when I desperately need the item, always to be soon replaced. These offerings do not expire and are usually material items such as jewelry, selected texts, or family heirlooms.

## Temporary offerings

Temporary offerings will be left out for a couple of days, or often a week or two. I prefer to give temporary offerings, such as flowers or non-perishable foods such as nuts, and dates. Of course, these offerings cannot last forever, but may be able to do so longer than expected.

## Perishable offerings

Perishable offerings are items that rot or evaporate over time such as water, foods, and desserts. These are meant to stay on the altar until they perish. I don't give food offerings unless I am eating something myself. I give food as an offering before I start eating and remove it from the altar after I finish eating.

Drinks are something I leave on the altar more than anything else, simply because they are easy, and the dead don't have drinks in the afterlife. The ancestors get fresh water, which is replaced every day.

## Acts of devotion

Acts of devotion aren't physical offerings. They are actions you perform in honor of the spirits. This could entail a variety of things, depending on what kind of spirit or entity you're giving offerings to.

Think about the spirit or entity that you are trying to honor. Think about what kind of hobbies they enjoyed. Think of the type of individual they are. This is something you really have to ponder for a moment.

For me, making jewelry is one way I feel connected to my ancestors. Many of the women in my family knew how to work metal and made a living from jewelry; it is a skill I picked up as well.

## Burnt offerings

Burnt offerings are things like candles and incense, tobacco, and so on. Personally, I prefer to burn some incense for my ancestors. It's a simple type of offering to give but I find many spirits like this. I imagine the smoke floating into the liminal space they exist within, and hope they enjoy the scent I have chosen for the day.

I also have pets, so I do not allow them near the incense when it is burning. Always make sure your pets aren't exposed to candles and incense. Make sure you open a window and have good ventilation.

Even if we do not know who our ancestors are, their spirit still exists within our existence. It is not necessary to identify who or where your ancestors came from in order to honor them. It is more than acceptable to simply honor them as "ancestors" and that is all. Our ancestors protect and comfort us from the other side. They are a part of our life even if we have never thought about their presence. Listen to them with your whole heart.

# COMMUNICATION

Spirits have the ability to protect and comfort from the other side. Conversely, they can also harm and put us in imminent danger. Be cautious about who you call upon. When calling for their attention, knock on a wooden table to gather the masses. We test these spirits by the way our hairs stand up on the back of our neck, and the way our gut twists and turns. Light a candle in their honor or renew their offerings if you wish to speak with a spirit. Most of the time, spirits will speak when they have something important to say.

Don't worry if you can't feel their presence, as my ancestors aren't even around most of the time. They only show up when they need to pass on information. Sometimes they'll demand attention, but other times they won't be around for days. Communication with spirits is an indirect process, and they won't always answer. However, we can still learn from an absent ancestor. Often in the simple act of veneration we are taught many, many lessons.

If a spirit feels that they need to help us in the afterlife, a piece of their soul will inhabit an item of a loved one's house—for example, a potted plant, kitchen pan, or maybe a pair of bellows. They choose to communicate with us via this "spirit object," providing us with knowledge and guidance. For example, Jinx's weeping fig would be considered a spirit object.

Often, the dead will contact us without our invocation, coming to us in dreams, smells, memories, and so on. This is them willing to connect with us, to make amends, to bring messages, and more. It is important to note you are not obligated to concede, but they do like to be acknowledged.

To dream of the dying isn't always a good thing, especially if the subject is alive. However, to dream of someone who has passed is a sure sign of spirit communication. Some folk have a gift for communicating with spirits in their dreams, being able to manipulate and control what happens in the dreamscape. This is what we call "dreaming right" or "dreaming true." It's hard to tell the difference between a regular dream and true dreaming. Fortunately, when you dream true, you always remember every single detail of it.

Most of the time when we dream, we're only left with an idea that something isn't right. I have solemnly dreamed true, recollecting only a few dreams of loved ones. My brother has always been visited by spirits and passed them in his dreams, and this gift is closely related to the sight. When you dream true, the dream won't be composed of symbolic meanings; it will be completely clear and comprehensible. Dreams are a one-way path for spirits and ancestors to deliver a message to us

without interference or intrusion from outside.

If a spirit is in less of a hurry, they might leave a more indirect sign, perhaps a reminder of something they loved in their lifetime. When a moth strays from its light, pay attention to where it is drawn instead. Strange dogs are said to bring messages from the dead, mostly with regard to illness or danger. There are many superstitions about what happens after we have passed away, my favorite being that when a witch is not laid to rest, they will turn into starlings and guide other practitioners to places of power with their swarms.

The starlings visited my home in the woods occasionally. When they showed up, I felt obligated to follow. I remember the first time I saw a swarm, I was so enchanted by its behavior that I just stood staring into the sky, quite unsure of what it was. Little did I know, those swarms would later bring me to the most powerful trees in the woods.

I once followed the starlings to a cemetery close by my family's property—a place where I have never felt such a pressing energy. It became one of the centers of my practice, and I have felt drawn to it ever since the day the starlings led me there. Cemeteries are ideal for spirit work, being a communal center for spirits and humans alike. Cemetery work takes a delicate touch, with many considerations and attentiveness put in place. Respect the dead and they will, perhaps, respect you.

# WHERE THE YEW BUSHES GROW

Cemetery magic is a common place to connect with the dead, as almost every town or village has a place for the dead to rest. Cemeteries exist in a liminal space, creating a strong place of power that can be used for a large array of magical workings, and of course ancestor veneration. The soul leaves the body at the time of death, but remains partially attached to the place where the body is buried. A fragment of their soul will always exist within this space, even if only to come and visit when needed.

In recent times, cemeteries have been viewed more as portals to the afterlife. They are enclosed by a fence or gate to contain the spirits of the cemetery who cannot wander past this designated area. The cemetery has multiple entrances, both physical and spiritual: Those at the entrance, the exit, and any other breaks in the gate. We work with spirits in the cemetery to connect with our ancestors, or make an exchange for them to do our or someone else's bidding.

Graveyards are the focus of many odd tales, and are a place of great importance in many cultures. A certain etiquette is required to maintain peace in the cemetery, as it is the designated area for the continued existence of souls on our physical plane.

When entering the cemetery, there is a widespread belief in giving an offering to the guardian of the cemetery in exchange for protection. The last person to be laid to rest is charged with keeping a watch on the surrounding area from sunrise to sunset. They are often a spirit who is new to the phenomenon of death. This guardian is discharged when the next person is buried. It's important to make sure that this spirit in particular is comfortable. They have recently passed, and may be suffering from grief themselves. Get to know the guardian, and they will help you through the cemetery.

When you enter a cemetery, raise your voice and announce your arrival. Visit the graves of children first, then adults and elders. If you eat, drink, or smoke in the cemetery, you must offer equal parts to the spirits. Do not take from the fenced area without permission from the guardian spirit. Never step on a grave, as it brings misfortune. Most of all, never allow a spirit to leave with you.

*No matter your offering, the spirits will appreciate the thought and work put into remembering and honoring them.*

## Cemetery offerings

A variety of offerings can be made when entering the cemetery, such as coins liquor, etc. Offerings are specific to different regions, cultures, and religions. For example, in my culture it is customary to leave rocks on headstones as a sign of gratitude and love. Whether you perform workings in the cemetery, or are just visiting, always bring an offering. While the dead will gladly accept any offering with true intention, sweets (cake, honey, cookies, candies), alcohol (vodka, red wine, rum), and coins (preferably pure silver or gold) can serve as universal offerings.

Adult spirits enjoy offerings of worldly indulgences. You can offer them lit cigars, pour alcohol over their grave, or bring them the food I just listed. Always make sure your offerings and behavior are respectful and appropriate to the surroundings. A child obviously requires different offerings: Toys, items of comfort, or sweet like cookies and jam.

If you know the subject of the grave you are visiting, use your intuition to choose an offering. Perhaps leave their favorite food, or an old item of theirs. No matter your offering, the spirits will appreciate the thought and work you put into remembering and honoring them. A spirit will rarely say your offering isn't good enough for their taste as long as you make your best effort.

The graves of children should always be tended to first, then those of elders, followed by those in between. After the familial graves are tended to, we move to the graves with worn names and mossy cracks, and we wash them. Always bring extra offerings for the forgotten dead. After you make an

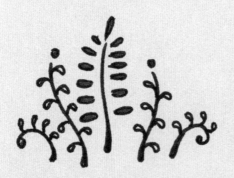

offering, you must establish contact and build a relationship with your ancestors or the soul of the deceased in order to complete any sort of task.

It should be said that not every spirit has our best interest in mind—even our ancestors, as they often use our efforts for their own personal machinations. Interacting with spirits safely and responsibly is a key factor in ancestor work. This must be mentioned:

Being dead doesn't make you a better person. The dead come back to us as they were in life, and they will exemplify these qualities as you work with them. If they were harsh and hateful in life, so will they be in death. If they were timid and shy, they'll be the same. That being said, it's always important to know who you're calling on, even among your ancestors.

# CHAPTER FOUR

# Living by the omens

**SIGNS AND SUPERSTITIONS**

Bees

Weather

Animals

Dreams

Household

# Signs and superstitions

THE SIGNS AND SUPERSTITIONS THAT LIVE IN THESE WOODS ARE A
COMMON WAY OF DISCOVERING THE CRAFT. WHETHER IT'S METHODICAL
PRECAUTIONS AGAINST BAD LUCK, OR HOW TO HEAL A BROKEN HEART,
THESE STORIES RUN WILD THROUGHOUT THE MINDS OF THE PEOPLE OF
THIS LAND. THESE SUPERSTITIONS AND THEIR REMEDIES HAVE BEEN
INSTILLED IN ME SINCE I WAS YOUNG, ESTABLISHING MY CORE BELIEFS
AROUND THEIR FAIR WARNINGS AND LESSONS.

Recognizing these omens and signs is key to thriving in the world. Many of these omens, strange as they are, are rooted in illness, death, and misery. These omens were made to explain the hardships of life— that which we cannot normally explain or fathom. While we often don't have to deal with the hardships of the old days, these superstitions have been passed down from generation to generation. The way I see it it's important to recognize the warnings these omens

hold in order to avoid the mishaps suffered by previous generations.

However, not all of these omens are necessarily about the bringer of death and illness, as some are simple and charming. My favorite superstition growing up was that when a witch sees another witch, she gets an immediate fit of loud hiccups. It always left me wondering how many I've met without knowing. Being prone to the hiccups, it would have amounted to a lot of witches. Many superstitions are as simple as they sound, having no plausible origin or cause. I was always told it's just how things are in this world. These omens often rely on what we already experience in life—weather, gardening, natural disaster, and so on. We learn to interpret the signs from the land around us, as the land is always most trustworthy. That being said, here I outline some of the most prominent superstitions in my life growing up. It should be mentioned that some of these omens carry more weight and significance than others, while others are once-in-a-lifetime occurrences.

## BEES

Growing up with a mother as a beekeeper, the bees were the providers of many omens and signs, indicating when the winds are changing, or telling us a storm is on the way. Bees are sacred beings, said to be able to fly between the physical and spiritual world. Because of this, they are a haven for meaningful messages. You must never injure a bee, as this will bring bad luck and bad health. Wasps are a different story.

However, we must care for the bees and actively interact with them to be able to interpret the signs they bring. That's why beekeepers are often seen as being so wise; the bees talk to them all day.

Talking to the bees is an important practice, as it's crucial to inform the bees of important events and changes in the family and home. If they aren't made aware of any situational changes, they might get angry and leave the hive. The bees always appreciate when you talk to them, as they have a lot to say. Doing so ensures you will have a happy hive that continues to grow. After all, their sound is hypnotic and not hard to listen to; it sounds a bit like summer heat to me. They have every right to sing while they gather pollen, as they work very hard to ensure the natural order stays exactly as it should.

That being said, the bees were the main source of interpretation for the future in our home. Oftentimes we would find a lone bee that had strayed from the hive flying around our house. This always meant we would soon have a visitor. Soon enough, somebody would visit us abruptly and unannounced. Always leave a window open for the bee to leave, or else your visitor will make sure to linger an annoyingly long time. On the other hand, if you wish to foster a relationship with somebody new, romantic or platonic, give them a jar of honey.

Bees also have a habit of letting us know when we've made a mistake. Being stung by a bee (not a wasp) indicates that there is some unfinished business left behind, or that we need to apologize to somebody. They are honest at heart and often get annoyed at our human tendencies for selfishness and ignorance. When trying to understand the bees, it's recommended you take care of any atonement that needs to be made, or else you're bound to get stung quite often.

# Uses of honey

Honey has a variety of uses; often helping bring prosperity and abundance. Below are some of my favorite uses for my mom's honey.

1  **Add to a spell to sweeten a situation**
2  **Mix into your tea and stir to the right for a positive day**
3  **Use in binding spells to "stick things together"**
4  **Leave as an offering to begin a relationship with a spirit**
5  **Eat a spoonful to soften your words**
6  **Place between two coins to invoke abundance**
7  **Drip on your doorstep to open the door to wealth**
8  **Feed to a lover to easily charm them**
9  **Apply to a burn to soothe the skin**
10  **Give to an enemy to soften their anger**

# WEATHER

In a world filled with mysteries and unidentifiable forces, the weather was often blamed for such occurrences and events. Without any other scientific explanation, this led the old folks to believe that just about everything meant something or other. A certain moon phase might be the best time to start a relationship, or even the best time to get married. One mistake in interpreting these signs could result in danger to the family and home.

Some country women believe that chickens are somehow able to predict what the weather will be like several days in advance. When chickens or turkeys stand with their backs to the wind, so that their feathers are ruffled, a storm is on the way. If hens spread their tail feathers and oil them conspicuously, it is sure to rain very soon. When a chicken bathes in the dust, the weather will be fair.

My mother is able to predict the weather through the aches and pains in her body, a skill that I, unfortunately, inherited. To feel the weather is to feel constant aches whenever the winds change or the tide rises. Achy knees mean a muddy, rainy day. Pain in the elbows means high winds. And an achy back simply means a cloudy sky is ahead.

There are lots of omens surrounding the winter storms and frosts, one of the most common being a sailor's warning: A red sky in the morning will mean a particularly harsh day of snow. On the other hand, if the dawns are short, then spring is near. Hearing thunder in February is said to signal a late frost. And the morels, the wise men of the woods, always graciously tell us the weather. If the morels grow scarce, a lengthy winter is in store. Listen for the low grumble of thunder for signs that it's time to come home. And August fog will always bring early snow.

Fog is quite an important aspect of the folk magic of the north, creating a liminal space in everyday areas. Its concealing nature brings the feeling of the unknown and the unseen. When the fog comes rolling in, it generally means the spirits want to talk and they will take the opportunity afforded by fog to do so. Fog is also useful if you wish to cast or enchant items such as necklaces for invisibility and protection while traveling.

*To feel the weather is to feel constant aches whenever the winds change or the tide rises.*

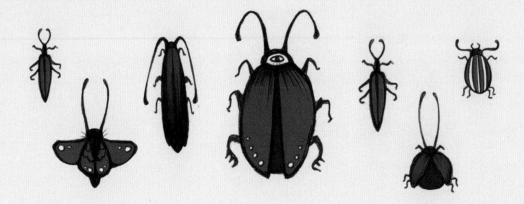

# ANIMALS

Animals have a knack for being able to pass over into the spirit world, often retrieving and presenting us signs in an uncanny way. These animals were believed to be conduits for divine beings to communicate with human beings. Some animals are considered more significant than others and encounters with them were often the source of many of the omens associated with the land. Here are some of the most important omens.

Occasionally you will hear a story about a healer who can turn into a white animal: A doe or fox or similar. Anyone coming in contact with one of these divine animals was expected to pay heed to the encounter and look for some changes in their near future. A white deer is a symbol of a direct message from the divine; however, seeing one in the spring is a sign of a bad planting season ahead.

## Insects and small creatures

Certain animals are capable of providing detailed nuances and distinctions. For example, if you ask a daddy longlegs (or cranefly) where to find a lost object, he will point the way with his longest leg. Seeing a daddy longlegs in the evening is a good thing, foretelling fortunes, happiness, and hope, but killing one will always bring rain the next day. Take note that this can be particularly useful if you need crops to grow in a drought. Snails have been known to spell out your future lover's name at dawn in the mud. A black snail is very unlucky to meet first thing in the morning, but a white snail brings good fortune. The smallest of animals often have the most to tell us.

## Birds

Birds are beings from above, carrying messages down from the stars. Generally, if a bird flies into the house, there will be major changes to the family that lives there. However, each species of bird brings different omens and meanings. The great pileated woodpecker is said to be a bird of the spirit world, with supernatural powers often valued by old folks. A woodpecker coming to your window means a wish is soon to be granted. Feed these woodpeckers and they will regularly bring you sweet messages. Seeing an owl in the road is not such a friendly sign, as it means that there is jealousy or bad intent being sent your way. On another unpleasant note, hearing a whip-poor-will while sick means the bird is trying to snatch your soul.

## Aquatic animals

Living by the lakes and swamps, waterfowl and other aquatic animals have a knack for interpreting the future. Being in close contact with bodies of water often gives them a heightened sense of the weather, due to the dominance of lakes over the climate.

If a beaver dam is built thick and heavy, blocking larger volumes of water than in years past, you can be sure the winter will be hard. The sighting of a water snake is enough to incite immediate change in the discoverer, as these animals only really make appearances when they need to. I was always told to thank every single fish you catch, for if you forget, your fish will tell the others you're very rude.

And by the way, fish won't bite when you're fishing under a Pisces moon.

# DREAMS

Many omens come to us at night in the form of dreams and nightmares. There are numerous correspondences from endless sources about dream interpretations, but these are what I've gathered from family knowledge over the years.

Dreams are often the forebears of troublesome times ahead. I've found that there will definitely be a time when a dream will tell you something good. An uncommon example is a dream of childbirth.

This sign is always welcome, being a foretelling of a happy and prosperous marriage. On the other hand, to dream of money means that the dreamer will be poorer than ever before. A dream of dying is usually a bad thing, but only if the dream comes at night, and oddly enough usually signifies a wedding gone bad. But, to fall asleep in the daytime and dream of death is very fortunate. And to dream of water, particularly a lake, means times are about to change.

> A dream of dying is usually a bad thing, but only if the dream comes at night, and oddly enough usually signifies a wedding gone bad.

# HOUSEHOLD

Your house is an individual being with its own consciousness. There is a reason why there are many stories of healers that live in homes filled with liveliness. Our home carries our energy, the energy of those before us, and those before them. The closer you grow to your home, the greater your bond will be. The house will give you tell-tale signs of the past, present, and future, that is if you make the effort to get to know your home.

An indication of signs in the home is often seen in the falling of spoons. When a spoon falls to the ground, it's a sign of visitors soon to come. If the spoon that has fallen is particularly small, then the visitor will either be a child or someone who is rather naive. On the other hand, if a soup spoon falls, then get ready to see a whole lot of family. The dropping of a serving spoon happens when someone very important is coming to your door. And a tablespoon means a baby is on the way.

A fork can give you more specific answers, meaning that a friend will soon be coming into your life. Whereas if a knife drops, a friend will soon be leaving. If you drop a fork and a knife at the same time, and they end up crossed, expect bad luck.

The way that a utensil falls is also very important in the interpretation of signs. A utensil pointing upward indicates your visitor is bringing good omens. If it's facing down, it means that they will bring disagreements, ill wishes, or simply bad news. And sideways always means a surprise. If you're like me and prefer not to have any visitors, don't drop your spoons.

# Part Two

# PRACTICAL FOLK MAGIC

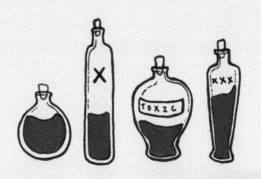

# CHAPTER FIVE

# Sticks, stones, and bones

## THE ART OF DIVINATION

### Throwin' the bones

### Tasseography

### Scrying

# The art of divination

WHEN DIVINATION COMES TO MIND, WE THINK OF CRYSTAL BALLS AND PLAYING CARDS. WHAT WE FAIL TO RECOGNIZE IS THAT DIVINATION IS ALL AROUND US, FROM HOW WE INTERPRET THE WEATHER, TO FLIPPING A COIN. THE OLD FOLK WERE FILLED WITH FEAR OF THE UNKNOWN. BY FOLLOWING SIGNS AND LISTENING TO THE SPIRITS, THE ELDERS WERE ABLE TO DISCERN THE FUTURE AND INTERPRET THE PAST.

Fortunes of love, a new job opportunity, or a person's true intentions can be uncovered through different methods. While some are complex and require practice, others are for the asking of a simple yes or no question and can be done on the fly. There are both complex and simple forms of divination; however, they all yield the same result: Insight. The essence of divination begins with simple probability, so let's start there.

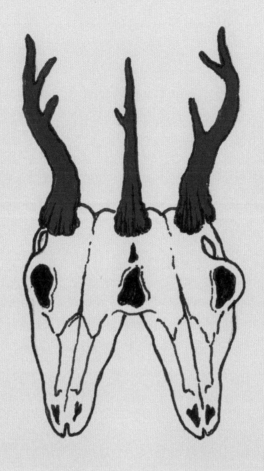

## THROWIN' THE BONES

Bone throwing is a deep practice, as it naturally employs the spirits of the bones you are using. While you can purchase these bones, I've always resonated best with the bones I've found naturally in their resting place. Throwing the bones is one of the oldest forms of divination on earth. It can be found in almost every culture, in many different forms using different techniques. Some readers use an array of bones, some utilize over a hundred pieces, and some as few as three. Some readers use charms in addition to bones, while others add nuts, shells, and other natural objects. Bone scrying is a very varied form of divination. Similar to other forms of scrying, the object that you see acts as a conduit of energy, working through you and capable of mimicking decisions, predictions, and actions.

However, the twist to bone throwing is that the bones are not only a conduit for your energy, but also the energy of the spirit of the bones. That is why when you are looking to take up bone throwing, it's

> *Rabbit energy is extremely lucky and prosperous, while fox energy is pretty mischievous down to the bone.*

important to foster a relationship with the bones and their spirits. Certain animal energy can affect specific divinatory matters. For example, rabbit energy is extremely lucky and prosperous, while fox energy is pretty mischievous down to the bone.

## How to throw the bones

When you use bones to tell the future, the results you are interpreting involve both your energy and the bone's energy. Bone throwing allows us to look into our own personal intuition, as well as gaining guidance from spirits.

A classic way to gain insight is to gather three long bones equal in length, such as femurs. Ponder your question and throw these bones onto the ground. You can wrap the bones in string or leather to provide a cushion or use an animal hide to break their fall. When you read the bones, look at whether they're crossed or not. Crossed bones means yes, while uncrossed means no.

## Bone-throwin' kits

The more bones you add to your throwin' kit, the more complicated your interpretations get. It's common to include other curiosities in bone throwing too. Your bones' meanings can be as specific as you want, or have no meaning at all. The bones are often thrown onto a cloth with marked symbols, an animal hide, the ground, or a table. Symbols and lines may be scratched or drawn onto the throwing surface to divide the casting space into meaningful areas.

I won't get into the nuances of bone throwing past

yes or no questions, as the best teacher for these types of practices is yourself. It provides a more personal and intimate connection with your practice. Besides, bone-throwing techniques are so diverse that you're unlikely to find anyone who practices the same way.

In my bone-throwin' kit, each bone has an assigned meaning according to its metaphysical properties. For example, a rabbit's foot might represent the inner child, while a fox tooth could represent the intuition.

## Bone-throwin' kits

Here's a list of my current bone-throwin' kit and each item's meaning:

### Three fox leg bones

*Used to determine yes or no answers. Throw the bones onto a flat surface and determine their positioning.*

### Fish vertebrae

*Symbolize decision making. Can also be used for yes or no answers with the flip-a-coin method.*

### Bobcat humerus

*Represents relationships and communication.*

### Prairie dog leg bone

*Embodies the home and family.*

### Coyote molar

*Detects the energy of an area or situation.*

### Deer antler

*To provide a vessel of communication for my spirit guides.*

### Snake vertebrae

*Represents self and identity.*

# Bone-throwin' oil

**½ cup (125 ml) grape seed oil**
**2 drops lavender oil**
**7 sandalwood flowers**

This oil is used to anoint and awaken bones used for divination. Often when we find bones, they've been laying around for quite some time. Cleaning them and applying a bone-throwin' oil helps awaken the spirit that resides in the bones. Simply mix together the oils and herbs and then apply them to the bones. Wipe off any excess oil and place your bones in a safe resting place.

My pieces speak to me individually through their stories: My antler, which once belonged to my great-grandfather; the tooth that was found in the woods; the fish bone from my childhood beach. Slowly the pieces of my kit presented themselves to me. Each time, these pieces would demand inclusion, stating clearly what they represent. However, despite my eagerness to learn, my first reading was … miserable. Trying to make sense out of nonsense is not easy. Many people avoid this sort of divination because it's seen as difficult, and it is. It is very intuitive and not terribly concrete; however, the amount of work you put in will be rewarded in the development of your practice.

# TASSEOGRAPHY

Reading tea leaves can be as simple or as intricate as your imagination makes it. But attention to detail makes all the difference. It's important to note that while tea-leaf reading is known for its fortune-telling aspects, it's also used to gain insight on the present and past.

The art of identifying symbols and interpreting messages is based on the concept of directing energy. When we focus our intention into the tea as we drink, the leaves become capable of mirroring our thoughts, behaviors, and experiences. When given intention and direction, the leaves can reveal blockages and offer advice and comfort.

Before you make yourself a cup of tea, keep in mind that different blends of tea will yield different results. The properties of the herbs can aid in your divination—for example, mint is used for enhanced insight and lavender when you're attempting to analyze the meanings of your dreams. My favorite tea for tasseography is chamomile, as it puts me into a state of association where my mind is free to roam. If you're tempted to cut open a tea bag, it will not yield the most accurate results. The tea is too finely ground and uniform in size to create varied images. Invest in loose-leaf tea.

Place the leaves directly into your cup and fill it with water (no need for strainers or infusers). While the leaves steep, focus on your intention. Take this time to reflect and transfer your energy into the cup. I prefer to let my tea steep for as long as I need to think or formulate a solid question; however, it is ultimately up to the tea-drinker. It is not necessary to formulate

a clear and concise question unless you wish to. The leaves will tell you things you need to know if what you seek is simply general insight.

## How to read the leaves

This is my general procedure for reading the leaves:

**1** *Pick up your cup (one that is preferably light-colored so you can read easily) in your non-dominant hand and focus deeply. Ask your question, if you have one. Turn the cup counterclockwise five times, then drink your tea.*

**2** *Once you have drunk your tea and the leaves remain at the bottom, turn the cup upside down on the saucer and allow it to drain. I always remain silent during this process, as reading the future can be quite a serious business.*

**3** *Once the cup has drained completely, turn it over, pick it up, and look at the patterns. Do not try to identify specific shapes yet. Allow yourself to dream a bit and instead ask yourself …*

What is my first impression? Is the cup full or empty? Are the leaves at the top or bottom, or both?

Read the cup in a clockwise direction beginning at the handle; the handle represents you, so the symbols closest to it are especially meaningful. Imminent events are found by the rim. Always begin with this area of examination because it is key to the rest of the reading.

The different areas of the cup suggest a timeline, giving us hints and clues as to the context in which the reading is set. The rim represents the immediate present and future, perhaps a day or so in advance. The middle, a little further into the future, may be a week ahead. And the base represents time that is further away, a week to a few months.

Numbers have a tendency to appear in the bottom of the cup. This often signifies a number of weeks or months before an important or meaningful event. This could be up to any imaginable time in the future. Readers often say "within a three," for example, meaning, three weeks, months, or years before an event takes place. The event itself will often be symbolized by a picture or a shape that appears next to the number.

Turn the cup around until you are able to discern a meaningful picture. Use the handle as your fixed point. Never strain to make sense of a cup that won't divulge its secrets. It may simply just not be the right time for a reading. Open up your mind's eye as you would while you are cloud gazing. Allow your inner child to play and discover meanings within symbols as you identify images in your cup.

Generally, you'll encounter animals, objects, letters, and numbers. These forms will be extremely obvious when the time is right. If you are more practically-minded, invest in a guide to tea leaf symbols—there are some out there with hundreds of depictions. There are general meanings to identify in your cup; however, I find it more beneficial when interpretation is done by intuition.

It is important to acknowledge that not every symbol has a meaning. Pay attention to what speaks to you and what you are drawn to. Symbols that stick out to you will prove important, while those that fade into the background symbolize insignificant happenings. Tasseography is all about your own internal reflections, as what you see is a direct manifestation of yourself.

# SCRYING

Scrying refers to a wide array of divinatory practices, from cloud watching to looking into an enchanted candle flame, the most famous being gazing into a crystal ball. Scrying allows us to let our mind wander until our intuition is in control. You'll see symbols and incoherent messages as you gain skills in scrying. Learning to translate these symbols takes time and practice. You might feel like your mind is just making you see things that aren't there, and I suppose on some level this is correct. The scrying material itself, whether it be smoke, water, or flame, isn't what's producing the vision. Ultimately, you are using the scrying material as a tool to help perceive such messages or visions.

## Swamp scrying

Swamp scrying is my preferred method of gazing, and is best done in a muddy puddle or swampy waters. However, most folk do it in a kitchen bowl. First, find some swampy water and gaze into it, letting your eyes lose focus. Your vision might get a little blurry, but try to fight the urge to look around and refocus. After a while of doing this, you might be able to correct the blurriness without losing your focus on the water. Around this point, when your gaze softens, some kind of vision should appear in the water. Interpretating what you see comes down to your intuition, as well as how your ears ring and hairs stand on end. What you feel when you swamp scry is the answer to your question.

Scrying allows us to let our mind wander until our intuition is in control. You'll see symbols and incoherent messages as you gain skills in scrying.

## Candle scrying

Candle scrying is a bit more complicated, as we're not only interpreting the images and figures we see in the flame, but how the flame reacts and behaves. A low flame means you should reconsider or do more thinking on the topic at hand. A high, steady flame indicates "yes." A rather weak flame should be regarded as a "no." A dancing flame often means that the universe holds a message for you. A violent, flickering flame indicates that a spirit is trying to pass through or communicate. If your candle will not light, now is not the time to consult the flame. However, if your fire won't go out, there's a lot to be learned in that scrying session.

Wax combines both aspects of candle and water scrying by pouring hot wax from your candle into water and then interpreting what you see. When we scry with wax, it is often similar to tea-leaf reading in the sense that the wax acts as a conduit of our energy and intention. To wax scry, light a candle and allow the wax to pool while you focus on your intent. Once enough wax has accumulated, pour it into your water bowl and allow it to to solidify. As the wax enters the water, it will form different shapes that you can interpret.

Numbers can indicate days, weeks, months, or even years. Letters can be clues to a person's name or place. A circle could indicate the end of a cycle, such as a completed project. A cluster of dots might indicate a group of people. If there is one formation sitting a distance from the rest of the drippings, it could represent isolation or going off on a distant trip. There are no right or wrong ways to interpret the candle wax, or any scrying subject for that matter.

## Bean scrying

The final form of scrying I use is bean scrying, by which I mean throwing beans on the ground and listening to what they say. The method of bean throwing you prefer might affect the types of beans you buy. A good thing to note is that beans are generally pretty cheap. For example, if you choose to scry, smaller beans work best for clearer images. If you're going to inscribe your beans, shoot for something bigger.

There are 41 throwing beans in a traditional set. Pick beans that are about the same shape, and avoid any cracks or imperfections. You are going to want the most perfect set possible. For a yes or no answer, you can simply throw the beans on a table, and split them evenly down the middle. Count the number of beans on each side. If the right side has more beans it's a "yes," and if the left side has more beans, it's a "no." And, well, if there is an even number on each side, the beans simply don't know.

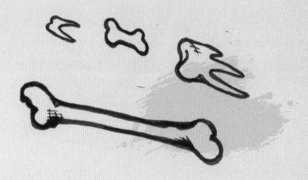

# CHAPTER SIX

# Wortcunning

## WILD MEDICINE

### Herbs

### Elemental herbs

### The magical uses of herbs

### Teas, brews, and infusions

# Wild medicine

IT'S THE WILD MEDICINE, THE FRUITS OF THE CROPS AND THE OLD
WISDOM THAT ENSURED THE SUCCESS OF GENERATIONS BEFORE ME THAT
CONTINUALLY DRAW ME IN. THE TOOLS USED IN THE CRAFT ARE THOSE
WE ALREADY HAVE, OR CAN EASILY FIND. THEY ARE AN EXTENSION OF THE
LIFE AROUND US, SIMPLY EXISTING WITHIN THEIR OWN EQUAL POWER.

Many belong to Mother Earth. No need to go buy something you can find outside. However, every time we take from the earth, we must see this interaction as a moment of blending between worlds. I always tell her what it will be used for and why I am taking her fruits. Doing so is simply an act of thankfulness for her endless bounty. I never take more than one tenth of what I find to leave room for growth for future generations.

However, a lot of tools are those you can find in your kitchen; most of the time, the ingredients you see there are the most versatile. The one thing I remember about my childhood kitchen is the number of plants that grew on the windowsill. My mother had never bought these plants, as they were always gifted to her or stolen. By stolen, I mean she'd pluck a neighbor's fruit, dry the seeds, then planted them, or find a lone vine on the floor of a greenhouse.

She said gifted plants grow best. She told me that these plants protected our household and everything inside of it, including me. When a plant died, it had done its job in protecting us. This is an example of how everyday belongings can be turned into powerful, magical objects.

That being said, none of these tools are necessary; they might, however, make the job a little easier.

I *never take more than one tenth of what I find to leave room for growth for future generations.*

# HERBS

I'm favorable to forest herbs. There's something about them that captivates me more than the cultivated varieties. I believe it's because I see parts of myself in these wild beings, as though they are a mirror for me to deepen my own understanding of myself. I'm drawn to them because they have what I long for—a connection to wildness, nature, and healing. They also connect me with the grief I carry, because I have become more domesticated than I would like to admit. Or maybe it's because our dominant culture sees these wild plants as weeds, and I feel they're not given the respect they're worthy of as fellow beings, with their own desire to express life in their particular form.

I'm also drawn to these herbs because they make the best herbal medicines. Over the years, I've become an amateur herbalist, and it's one of the greatest joys of my life. Many wild plants can be used to make tinctures, teas, infused oils, lotions, salves and more to help us heal all sorts of physical ailments. They can ease rashes and stomach aches, remove the pain from bee stings, help us heal broken bones faster, and so much more. Some wild plants can also support us emotionally—they can lift our troubled mind from a stressful day, or nurture a broken heart in times of grief. The blessings these herbs offer us is profound.

However, one of the ways a plant can heal is through its magical properties. Each plant's energy is unique in its own way, and there are many beliefs around metaphysical uses through different cultures and lands. Plants have great knowledge to share with us, if only we open ourselves up to the idea of treating plants as subjects rather than objects.

In creating this connection with a plant, we are introduced, in one way or another, to the ideology of the plant spirit. By acknowledging the omniscient presence of the plant, we recognize that they are vital living creatures who retain their power in both life and death, as a root, an incense, a dried herb … Most believe that spells and herbal concoctions are similar to chemistry. However, some understand that the most important facet of a spell is, in fact, this subtle force of the plant spirit. It is the bond between our spirit and that of the plant's that is the catalyst behind magic.

To create this bond, many cultivate a garden or tend to the wildlife around them. Others may cook and ingest the plants they are working with. Of course, creating a relationship with a plant can work

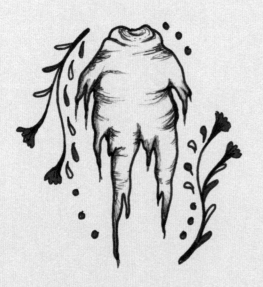

exclusively on the spiritual level, revolving around communication and intermediary lessons. The key to this work is to not "give" the plant any energy, but simply to mingle its energy with your own; to speak to it, to commune with its autonomous spirit, and tell it what you want in personal terms. As a spirit, the plant has its own wants and needs; and as a practitioner, working with the plant includes meeting these wants and needs in your work. If you listen to the plant, it will tell you exactly how to use it.

On the other hand, many will physically woo the plant, offering it gifts and flattering it with compliments until the herb chooses to return the favor. This implies that a consciousness exists within the plant that can receive and respond to messages from our world to theirs. While every practitioner interacts with each plant in a different manner, this group soul, or existing consciousness within the species or type of plant, usually tends to appear with recurring prominent characteristics—some would even say different personalities.

It is through these distinct personalities that we learn lessons from a plant, herb, flower, or root. As with the people around us, we are drawn and repelled by certain characteristics. I have found in my observations that the plants we tend to be most attracted to exhibit the attributes we most need to adjust within ourselves. I have always been particularly interested in plants with a trickster spirit—datura in particular. And while the tricksters do love some good fun and games, they are always wreaking havoc, and always causing change—change being an idea I have always struggled to embrace.

By having datura as a plant guide, I am actively learning to accept change as it comes, observing how the datura spirit does so easily.

In order to understand the characteristics and personality of the plant, we must observe its habitat and its traditional folklore and growth cycles. Sometimes the plants in the forests of the north are assigned properties in the simplest manner—for example, by observing the physical attributes of the plant, so that a rose is seen as protective because of its many thorns, for example. Recognized medicinal properties of herbs can give a strong indication of their magical uses as well. Yarrow clots blood and seals wounds, in a similar way to how you can use yarrow to heal wounds affecting your own personal energy system.

Through these physical characteristics and growth patterns, we are able to observe the elements corresponding to each plant that grows. Through elemental correspondences, we are able to attribute planetary correspondences, and so forth.

Planetary influences help us order and conceptualize the world differently from the way we usually do. Certainly, when working with plants we notice that particular properties and characteristics tend to occur in sets that do not coincide with the separate boxes that mainstream science offers.

# ELEMENTAL HERBS

I've found that herbs can be categorized by the elements and their planetary influence. Perceiving plants from the perspective of their elemental and planetary influence can show us relationships between plants and their uses that we would otherwise miss.

Elemental herbs give us a basic understanding of the concept of that specific plant spirit. The plant spirit world is expansive, and often lies outside of the reach of our understanding. Assigning elemental correspondences to the herbs and plants we interact with allows us to conceptualize these spirits on a level we are familiar with.

Furthermore, we must first be able to identify what element rules a plant in order to discern its planetary aspects. Again, look at the physical characteristics of the herb, such as its smell, taste, or simply color. Determining a plant's elemental correspondences should not be a struggle, and if need be, use the feeling deep in the pit of your stomach that tells you what is right and what is wrong. After all, herbalism is an intuitional practice.

## Fire

A plant associated with the fire element might have a particular spicy taste, or it may have a warm scent. Red flowers and thorns are also a good indicator of fire rulership. They will also often bloom at midday, or during the height of summer. Fire plants often grow in fields or grassy plains, and are used in protective and energetic magic. They are often used to revitalize the soul, or accelerate a situation.

*The plant spirit world is expansive, and often lies outside of the reach of our understanding.*

## Water

Elemental water plants are a bit easier to identify, as they often grow in wetlands and swamps, or in lakes or ponds. Moon bloomers are almost always classified as water plants, due to the moon's associations with lakes, and they are often shades of blue and lavender. They frequently carry water internally, expressed by plump and succulent leaves. Water plants deal with areas of emotions and expression, including intuition and awareness.

## Air

Air plants are often morning bloomers, showing us their true colors early in the day. Spring plants are representative of air, as well as plants that have particularly fragrant scents. They often grow tall and thin, climbing and clinging to what they can. Air plants are frequently known to spread their seeds through the wind, rather than through pollination or other methods. Air plants are excellent when used in areas of learning and communication, as well as for stimulating creativity and the imagination.

*Air plants are excellent when used in areas of learning and communication.*

## Earth

Earth element plants are often categorized by the slow growers and fertility bringers. While we might categorize most plants as linked to the earth, only the most stabilizing and grounding of herbs fall under this class. These plants grow year-round, in the deepest of forests and deepest of valleys. Earth plants often grow hardy and deep roots, or have an "earthy" smell or taste. These plants are best used in areas around the home, for protection and grounding, as well as to promote health and good finances.

You must also pay attention to the way the plant grows once it is harvested, as not all herbs are suitable for magical workings. Looking at the plant's roots can give you a good indication of the effectiveness of the herb; if the roots are knotted and tangled, the working is likely to be rough going and complicated. But if the roots are smooth, the spell that is using the herbs will work. Some plants, such as morning glories, have naturally gnarly roots where the opposite is true for them: Gnarly is good; smooth is bad.

# THE MAGICAL USES OF HERBS

## APPLE

Apple is a powerful fruit that represents both fertility and immortality. Apples also serve as a principal ingredient in love potions and love divination, and are a powerful healing agent for metaphysical purposes. The fruit itself can be charged with healing or love powers and given to the subject later.

    Elemental Correspondence: Water
    Planetary Correspondence: Venus
    Energetic Direction: Projective

## AMARANTH

Being a plant of mental powers, it is said that wearing amaranth flowers helps our connection with the divine. It is most commonly used for spirit communication and connection with the journey of death. It is also a plant of immortality, and is often dried and added to spells to promote longevity.

    Elemental Correspondence: Earth
    Planetary Correspondence: Saturn
    Energetic Direction: Receptive

## ANISE

Anise stars are a divination aid, allowing us to open the intuitional centers of the mind. They can also help with enhancing the vividness of dreams, directing our consciousness to remember the details of greatest importance. Prosperity follows where anise is spread.

    Elemental Correspondence: Water
    Planetary Correspondence: Lunar
    Energetic Direction: Receptive

## ASPARAGUS

Asparagus is a potent love herb, often used to represent fertility and lust. Use asparagus as a powerful attracting agent, as well as to increase the potency of any spell it is added to. Traditionally, asparagus has also been used for increasing endurance and strength.

    Elemental Correspondence: Fire
    Planetary Correspondence: Venus
    Energetic Direction: Projective

## BASIL

Most commonly associated with the amassing of wealth, basil is also used in love workings. This herb can be carried in your pockets to attract wealth or kept in cash registers, or grown by the door to attract business. In the context of love, basil is primarily concerned with seduction and lust. I have also heard of the spirit of basil being a frequent aid in astral travel.

    Elemental Correspondence: Fire
    Planetary Correspondence: Mars
    Energetic Direction: Projective

## BAY LEAF

Bay is a manifestation herb. The most commonly known method is to write your manifestation on the leaf itself and then burn it whole. Specifically, bay leaves are best for prosperity and pursuit of metaphysical and material wealth.

    Elemental Correspondence: Fire
    Planetary Correspondence: Jupiter
    Energetic Direction: Projective

## BIRCH

*The old folk would use birch water to attract the energies needed for protection, purification, and the exorcism of evil. Many believed that the spirits of their dead ancestors lived within birch and that it was the greatest tree in the world.*

**Elemental Correspondence: Earth**
**Planetary Correspondence: Saturn**
**Energetic Direction: Projective**

## BLACKBERRY

*A herb of safety in love, blackberries are specifically used for preservation and protection of relationships. The thorns can be used to represent protection, while the fruit represents the heart, filled with love. Often used in binding spells, blackberry is a useful herb for boundaries in romance as well.*

**Elemental Correspondence: Water**
**Planetary Correspondence: Venus**
**Energetic Direction: Projective**

## CALENDULA

*Calendula represents the sun. I've found it most useful for bringing light and happiness to situations, and for exposing the truth in particular. Calendula is powerful when used in situations associated with the law, gambling, as well a those that require a sway of odds.*

**Elemental Correspondence: Fire**
**Planetary Correspondence: Solar**
**Energetic Direction: Projective**

## CATNIP

*Just as cats enjoy indulging in catnip, this herb can be used to bring relaxation and positivity to otherwise stressful situations. Catnip is a balancing herb, particularly useful for providing protection from nightmares and spirits during rest or sleep.*

**Elemental Correspondence: Water**
**Planetary Correspondence: Venus**
**Energetic Direction: Receptive**

## CHAMOMILE

*The energy of chamomile primarily deals with purification. In that sense, it is very useful as a means of relaxation and meditation. Making chamomile tea before bed was a ritual in my childhood, and I was unable to sleep peacefully without it.*

**Elemental Correspondence: Fire**
**Planetary Correspondence: Solar**
**Energetic Direction: Receptive**

## CINNAMON

*Cinnamon is an intensifying agent, often used in pairings with herbs of love and money. It is attracting, pulling in our desires, wants, and needs. Cinnamon can also be used for purification and cleansing, as cinnamon broomsticks are often made to sweep negative energy out the door.*

**Elemental Correspondence: Fire**
**Planetary Correspondence: Mars**
**Energetic Direction: Projective**

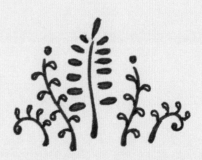

## CLOVES

*Often associated with protection and money, I've found cloves most helpful in the preservation of wealth. Cloves can be used to draw money in and keep it safe.*

> **Elemental Correspondence: Earth**
> **Planetary Correspondence: Jupiter**
> **Energetic Direction: Receptive**

## COMFREY

*Comfrey is a versatile herb, often used for everything from divination to cleansing and fortune telling. However, I've found it most effective in offering protection from negative energies and entities. Use comfrey while traveling to guard against misfortunes, injury, and illness.*

> **Elemental Correspondence: Earth**
> **Planetary Correspondence: Jupiter**
> **Energetic Direction: Projective**

## DAMIANA

*This is a herb of spiritual enhancement and divinatory awareness. Damiana is also a potent aphrodisiac, often used in love charms. It can help us find peace within ourselves and simplify the flow of our thoughts.*

> **Elemental Correspondence: Water**
> **Planetary Correspondence: Venus**
> **Energetic Direction: Receptive**

## DANDELION

*Dandelion itself is a powerful herb for exertion of the will, as it centers around energy and its execution. A dandelion root can be carried with you to bring happiness, and use the flower in spellwork to enhance or speed up the process a bit.*

> **Elemental Correspondence: Fire**
> **Planetary Correspondence: Solar**
> **Energetic Direction: Projective**

## FENNEL

*Fennel is a herb of privacy, providing shelter and invisibility from nosy individuals. Use fennel when your affairs need to be kept quiet. It also bestows a certain elegance and suaveness on the user.*

> **Elemental Correspondence: Air**
> **Planetary Correspondence: Mercury**
> **Energetic Direction: Receptive**

## FERNS

*The fern often represents protection from the outside world (similar to fennel), providing shelter from harm under this plant's magic. The burning of a fern is said to summon rain, as well as protection from creatures of the wild and other invisible threats.*

> **Elemental Correspondence: Air**
> **Planetary Correspondence: Mercury**
> **Energetic Direction: Projective**

## FORGET-ME-NOTS

*Believed to strengthen the bonds between our heart and mind, this flower helps us to understand how the balance of these two elements contributes to overall happiness. Magically, the flower creates activity and helps unblock mental obstructions.*

> **Elemental Correspondence: Air**
> **Planetary Correspondence: Mercury**
> **Energetic Direction: Receptive**

## GHOST PIPES

*This ghostly plant represents the thin veil that exists between our world and the spiritual realm. It is particularly useful for transcendence; helping us understand the connection between physical and mental ailments. It has strong grounding properties as well, making sure we never float too far into unconsciousness.*

**Elemental Correspondence: Air**
**Planetary Correspondence: Mercury**
**Energetic Direction: Receptive**

## GINGER

*Ginger is an influential attraction herb, allowing us to draw in any desire we choose. Whether it be love, spiritual success, or money, ginger can be used in spells as a receptive herb. Its spirit is also highly protective of our emotions, making a great ward against heartbreak and emotional damage.*

**Elemental Correspondence: Fire**
**Planetary Correspondence: Mars**
**Energetic Direction: Projective**

## GOLDENROD

*Goldenrod is highly connected to the intuitional world, and is frequently used as a divinatory aid, either as incense, spellwork, or through other means. Wearing a goldenrod flower will supposedly help you divine your future lover within a fortnight.*

**Elemental Correspondence: Air**
**Planetary Correspondence: Mercury**
**Energetic Direction: Receptive**

## HYDRANGEA

*Hydrangea, both grown wild and as a commercial flower, can be used as a banishing and reversing agent. The flower can be used to return energy to its sender, as well as protect from further energetic sabotage.*

**Elemental Correspondence: Air**
**Planetary Correspondence: Saturn**
**Energetic Direction: Receptive**

## JASMINE

*Known for its flowers, jasmine is popular for its uses as a dreaming aid and as an ingredient in divinatory tea. It is also an attractive herb, specifically used for love. Jasmine can be carried in a sachet to enhance self-love and inner beauty, as well as used as an oil before meditation.*

**Elemental Correspondence: Water**
**Planetary Correspondence: Lunar**
**Energetic Direction: Receptive**

## JOE PYE WEED

*Joe Pye weed, frequently found growing in ditches and by roadsides, is specifically used to gain confidence and earn respect from others through improvement of our own actions. This herb can also be used to enhance the likelihood of your opinions being accepted by people who normally oppose you.*

**Elemental Correspondence: Earth**
**Planetary Correspondence: Jupiter**
**Energetic Direction: Projective**

*Use fennel when your affairs need to be kept quiet.*

## JUNIPER

Juniper is suitable for preventing nightmares and reversals, and providing cleansing. The juniper protects and purifies, removes bad remnants, and prevents their return. But don't use him wastefully. Contemplate and deliberate before asking his help, or he might just not assist you at all.

Elemental Correspondence: Earth
Planetary Correspondence: Saturn
Energetic Direction: Projective

## LAVENDER

Lavender is a calming herb, well known for its ability to calm and destress a situation. Lavender can be placed under the pillow to stimulate peaceful sleep with positive dreams. It can also be used as an oil or in spells to easily put yourself into the headspace for meditation and intuitional activities. Its aromatic fragrance is an easy way to calm our innermost thoughts.

Elemental Correspondence: Air
Planetary Correspondence: Mercury
Energetic Direction: Receptive

## LEEKS

This powerful protection herb grows abundantly on the forest floors. Carrying a leek is said to bring safety, while biting into one is a simple way to break a hex. It is said that those who eat leeks together will soon fall in love.

Elemental Correspondence: Fire
Planetary Correspondence: Mars
Energetic Direction: Projective

## LEMONGRASS

Capable of expanding limited horizons, lemongrass is a herb of understanding and deep spiritual awareness. Unlike other citrus scents, it is deeply calming, allowing us to open our mind to new avenues that we've never considered before.

Elemental Correspondence: Air
Planetary Correspondence: Mercury
Energetic Direction: Receptive

## MINT

Mint is most often used in money and prosperity workings; however, it can also be useful for opening up new possibilities. Frequently known as a road opener, mint is a change bringer, attracting abundance and good fortune into life. It can also aid in travel, providing safety while as we explore new opportunities.

Elemental Correspondence: Air
Planetary Correspondence: Mercury
Energetic Direction: Receptive

## MULLEIN

This magic herb has various connections to the idea of returning. Mullein leaves, with very little natural odor, provide a perfect base for incense blends related to death intuition. Mullein is always protective of the dreamer.

Elemental Correspondence: Earth
Planetary Correspondence: Saturn
Energetic Direction: Receptive

## MUGWORT

Mugwort is a powerful intuitional tool, which can be used in spells to harness lunar energy, as well as invite a spiritual connection with ourselves. Mugwort often gives a true reflection of the self, showing what we can do to improve in future.

Elemental Correspondence: Water
Planetary Correspondence: Lunar
Energetic Direction: Receptive

## MULBERRY

*The sweet berries of this tree represent the home, and familial workings are heavily tied to this tree. Hang mulberry branches around the home when looking to add a means of protection. The berries can also be made into a wonderful jam, which can then be gifted to a loved one to ensure their safety.*

Elemental Correspondence: Air
Planetary Correspondence: Mercury
Energetic Direction: Projective

## OREGANO

*Oregano is said to be a staple ingredient in love and luck workings. It is a joyful herb, adding prosperity and abundance when used to sweeten a situation. Growing oregano in the home is an easy way to promote material and spiritual wealth.*

Elemental Correspondence: Fire
Planetary Correspondence: Mars
Energetic Direction: Receptive

## PARSLEY

*Parsley is a herb of deep love and protection of said love. Wearing parsley is said to invoke fertility, and using it in a spell for lovers can solidify a relationship. Parsley can also be added to a sachet that is then soaked in a bathtub to create a cleansing wash that banishes the energy of past relationships.*

Elemental Correspondence: Fire
Planetary Correspondence: Mars
Energetic Direction: Receptive

## QUEEN ANNE'S LACE

*While the flower and leaves are famous for their uses in fertility workings and rites, their roots are notoriously lucky. Not just any Queen Anne's lace root, only one with a forked bottom. These roots are often worn as a talisman during the dog days.*

Elemental Correspondence: Earth
Planetary Correspondence: Mars
Energetic Direction: Projective

## RASPBERRY

*Raspberry's thorny branches teach us to be protective of the fruits of our labor. This is a herb of patience in fertility and love, and can be used in spellwork or rituals to invoke true feelings of self-love and worthiness.*

Elemental Correspondence: Earth
Planetary Correspondence: Jupiter
Energetic Direction: Receptive

## ROSES

*Roses carry a dual-edged sword of protection and seduction. The rose's scent is a powerful aphrodisiac, drawing us in; meanwhile its thorns draw blood if we mishandle the stems. Because of this double purpose, roses are best used to protect a relationship or a specific person's romantic career.*

Elemental Correspondence: Water
Planetary Correspondence: Venus
Energetic Direction: Receptive

## ROSEHIPS

*Rosehips are commonly harvested in the fall and winter and best used in relationship workings. They can be used to invoke new friendships or draw in a lover. As a symbol of fertility, rosehips are wonderful for promoting growth in relationships, especially when feelings or "the spark" seems to have diminished.*

Elemental Correspondence: Earth
Planetary Correspondence: Venus
Energetic Direction: Receptive

## ROSEMARY

*The spirit of rosemary is a protector of the home, the most important of all the things that are close and essential. Grow rosemary near the home to prevent negative energy from entering your property. Rosemary can also be burned to purify a space.*

Elemental Correspondence: Fire
Planetary Correspondence: Solar
Energetic Direction: Projective

## RUE

*Rue is a staple in protective magic. It was traditionally hung around the home to ward off negative energy, and worn to avert the evil eye. Rue is especially useful for providing safety while engaging in divinatory and psychic practices. It is also helpful when developing these practices, and strengthening your intuitional instincts.*

Elemental Correspondence: Fire
Planetary Correspondence: Solar
Energetic Direction: Projective

## SKULLCAP

*Skullcap is commonly used as a herb of magical bindings, boundaries, and loyalty. Use skullcap when looking to secure a situation, or gain further understanding of a challenging topic.*

Elemental Correspondence: Air
Planetary Correspondence: Mercury
Energetic Direction: Receptive

## SOLOMON'S SEAL

*This herb is named after King Solomon, and represents the wisdom he held. The root of this plant has potent effects when you are trying to retain knowledge and gain mastery of difficult skills. Solomon's seal is most effective when used in a school or workplace setting.*

Elemental Correspondence: Earth
Planetary Correspondence: Jupiter
Energetic Direction: Receptive

## STINGING NETTLES

*Although many people have heard of her sting, not many have heard of her kindness. Stinging nettles are used to bring good health and fortune. They have powerful healing benefits for both the body and soul. They can also be used to preserve and protect your health.*

Elemental Correspondence: Fire
Planetary Correspondence: Mars
Energetic Direction: Receptive

## ST. JOHN'S WORT

*I always collect St. John's wort on Fridays to ward off unhappiness. It's also a common staple in my house, as it is hung over the kitchen to protect against nasty weather. Use St. John's wort in a spell to increase potency as well as to bring joy to a struggling friend.*

Elemental Correspondence: Fire
Planetary Correspondence: Solar
Energetic Direction: Projective

## SUMAC

*Growing wild in fields and hillsides, the bright red berries of the sumac plant are very useful in love workings—both the breaking of love and the summoning and strengthening of* relationships. This plant is powerful for the reversal of romantic feelings, and can quickly incite hatred.

> Elemental Correspondence: Earth
> Planetary Correspondence: Venus
> Energetic Direction: Receptive

## SWEET PEA

The sweet pea plant grows wild and delicate, representing its ability to help us appreciate the little pleasures of life. This plant can be used in a spell to bring more joy and happiness in the activities we seek. At night, it can help promote peaceful, restorative, dreamless sleep.

> Elemental Correspondence: Water
> Planetary Correspondence: Jupiter
> Energetic Direction: Receptive

## TURNIP

The turnip is a banishing agent, able to remove and relocate energy from a variety of sources. Using turnips in your workings is a simple way to reverse or get rid of something that is sticking around longer than you would ideally like.

> Elemental Correspondence: Earth
> Planetary Correspondence: Saturn
> Energetic Direction: Projective

## VERVAIN

This herb is a truth bringer. Often used to bring light to the shadows and expose others' true intent, vervain is a common herb to find in the witch's cabinet. Using vervain in a spell is a fast way to reveal a friend's honesty, or to gain the loyalty of a trusted ally. Vervain can also be burned as a method of cleansing a space of deceptive energy.

> Elemental Correspondence: Water
> Planetary Correspondence: Venus
> Energetic Direction: Receptive

## YARROW

Yarrow has been long recognized as a generally protective and cleansing plant. It can be strung around the home as a ward, or burned to offer protection. Hanging yarrow above your doorway is said to keep unwanted guests at bay.

> Elemental Correspondence: Water
> Planetary Correspondence: Venus
> Energetic Direction: Projective

# TEAS, BREWS, AND INFUSIONS

## TEA

Pour boiling water over herbs and steep for 10–15 minutes.

## INFUSION

Pour boiling water over herbs and steep with lid for 4–6 hours or overnight for a stronger infusion.

# CHAPTER SEVEN

# Magical tools

## ON BONES, WANDS, AND DUSTS

### Bones

### Wands

### Dirts and dusts

### Shells

### Water

### Mushrooms

### Stones

# On bones, wands, and dusts

BONES, TREES, SHELLS, TYPES OF DUST, AND EVEN WATER CAN ALL HAVE
MAGICAL PROPERTIES. THIS CHAPTER LOOKS AT HOW TO HARNESS THEIR
MIRACULOUS POWERS AND WEAVE THEM INTO YOUR SPELLWORK.

## BONES

Bones are unique in the way they carry dualistic properties; that is, the spiritual properties of the animal they came from, and the magical correspondences that arise from the parts of the body concerned. Think of bones as living things, as you might a plant or tree.

Just as you would choose various plants for your workings based on their magical purposes—protection, love, money, and so on—so bones also have magical associations. Not all bones are used for the same thing: Snake energy in magic is very different from, say, fox energy. I tend to keep deer antlers around when doing spirit work, because deer are believed to be able to cross easily between realms.

The part of the body a bone comes from can also play a role in determining its magical properties.

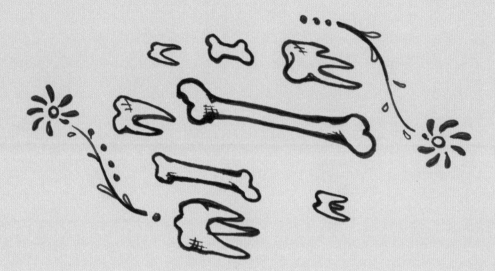

Skulls can be used for divination by gazing into the eye sockets or even into the base of the skull. Being the seat of consciousness, any images or messages received are thought to be from the spirit inhabiting the skull.

Looking into the energetic aspects of the placements of bones provides a powerful and one-of-a-kind energy. For example, wolves are known for their protective, loyal energies. A wolf skull would be ideal for spiritual protection, while a wolf leg would offer protection while traveling. Bones are diverse in their metaphysical uses, carrying dual meanings and mannerisms.

Furthermore, using an ankle bone in a work environment is a catalyst for change. They are a symbol of movement, specifically moving on. The antler is a messenger from the spirit work, aiding us in astral work as we venture into the unknown. Carrying an antler offers spiritual protection to the one who has bonded with it. An arm bone can be used for blocking others' spellwork; conversely, it is also one of the most useful bones for the helping and healing of others. Claws of all sorts are a very protective material, for both spiritual and physical endeavors.

Fingers and hand bones are excellent for speeding up a spell. You can also carry one of these bones to increase creativity and energy. A foot bone works in the same way, often helping you to manifest good luck and ensure safe travels. Hip bones are ideal for encouraging strength and stability. Horns are another bone of protection, often hung around the home to ward off spirits. The horn is a symbol of determination, as horned animals work very hard. Leg bones are a staple in travels, encouraging movement and change. Carrying a leg bone while you travel is said to guide you during a long journey.

Skulls, as mentioned before, are used in divination, spirit work, and workings involving the mind. Hanging a skull around the home is a way to increase communication and understanding of one another. A spine has entirely to do with asserting yourself, gaining confidence and value. Vertebrae can be carried for a simple boost in courage. A tail represents agility and adaptation, ruling over our ability to change with the wind.

Teeth are perhaps my favorite type of bone to use and carry, as they represent communication, protection, defense, and change. Teeth are particularly powerful in warding off bad dreams and nightmares, especially if placed under the pillow. The bones from toes increase our ability to balance the weight of the world, bringing in luck, and sometimes money. If you are fortunate enough to become the owner of a wing or a wing bone, you should be aware that they are known for attracting adventure and new travels. They can be used in spells concerning hope, comfort, and luck as well.

> Hanging a skull around the home is a way to increase communication and understanding of one another.

# WANDS

As a kid, I was an avid whittler. I was given a pocketknife and would sit and carve magic wands as my dad worked outside. Wands, staffs, and rods are special tools used in certain rituals. Wands are always made from a fallen tree branch, and finding such a tree branch should be thought of as a gift from nature. I personally never cut from the branch of a tree. Magic wands and staffs help to concentrate and direct your personal power. They are used to collect, store, direct, and finally release energy to and from a certain point. Although wood is traditionally used, wands and staffs may also be created from a variety of materials, including glass, clay, metal, or bone.

Magic wands made from wood are cut to the length of the owner's forearm. Staffs are commonly made about shoulder-length high. Since they can double as walking sticks, ensure they are thicker and more stable than a wand. A variety of trees are traditionally used to make magic wands and staffs, each with a different property, in the same way as herbs. Most wands are made out of oak, willow, or elder wood; however, there is a large array of magical woods to use on your whittling adventures.

Alder wood is represented by fire and water. It brings us the ability to balance passion and calm, attracting and banishing. It's an ideal wood for balancing and working with all the elements. Ash wood also holds a certain duality, shown in the fact that it is both physically and magically healing. Owning an ash wand is said to bring luck whenever used. The aspen is the tree of rebirth, helping us overcome life obstacles and barricades. She is a shield to those who utilize her magic.

Beech wood is particularly friendly. Ruled by mercury, beech wood enhances our communication, especially with spirit work. Beech trees are often said to grant wishes to those who water and trim them. However, birch wood is aggressive in nature, helping us to banish hexing and other baneful measures and for providing protection.

Cedar is the most cleansing of all the woods, and can be burned in the home to banish both good and bad energy. It is said to help promote a peaceful demeanor and aid in interpreting messages from the higher self. Cherry trees are found scattered across the land, her wood sweet and savory. A cherry wand is fit for fertility and love workings, but can also be used for the occasional healing.

Dogwood is often used in protected amulets, and a wand made of dogwood can be used very similarly. Dogwood encourages us to strengthen our intuition to avoid troublesome interactions in the first place.

Elm wood is centered around stability and ensuring longevity and strength to the owner. Elm can be used

specifically to promote the empowerment of the divine feminine. Reputed to be very lucky, elder wood is trickier to master. When tamed, the elder is a powerful tool in protection and banishing. When an elder grows near the home naturally, it will protect the family of that home.

Fir trees are used to bring out the truth, and can be extremely useful when gaining insight via divination. The ginkgo is said to be the wisest of them all, and symbolizes longevity of the mind, body, and spirit. It contains high magical energy, drawing out and strengthening our powers of intuition.

Hazel wood is the holder of knowledge, being a great tool when learning or acquiring new skills. The hazel tree is a teacher, enjoying spreading her words of wisdom. Ironwood trees are unbreakable, and teach us the strength to be found in kindness. She will shield us under her powerful branches.

Hickory trees are playful, teaching us the strength to be gained from flexibility. Similar to that of the oak, a hickory wand puts our mind at rest and brings out the energy deep inside us. Hemlock is a master of the unknown, aiding us in divination as well as spirit and astral work. A hemlock wand is ideal for the experienced witch, who is not afraid of its power.

The maple tree is kind enough to let us extract her sap when the season comes, symbolizing the change of seasons and decision-making. The old oak tree is a master of healing, helping us feel at ease and become the best version of ourselves. Using an oak wand can greatly aid in healing rites and rituals of the mind and body. Then there are the pine trees, standing tall and strong. They teach us to find

comfort in isolation and security in our lonesome. A pine wand is best used by a solitary witch who solemnly has company.

A popple (poplar) tree is a holder of success, granting wishes to whoever he sees worthy. He has foresight into the future, and is never wrong in his assumptions. The rowan tree is the most mystical of them all, holding his secrets deep. He is a protector against evil and all unwanted energy. Owning a rowan wand will bring security in the light of mysteriousness. The lone sumac standing in the field represents the energy of the wilderness itself. It carries striking berries and blood-red leaves in the fall, and wood that can be used to speak to the strong man of the woods.

The willow tree is renowned for its sense of hope, being able to provide a feeling of belonging to those that seek her comforts. She carries lunar energy, symbolizing the transition from life to death. The old walnut tree is a symbol of growth, aiding us as we gain knowledge through our studies. A walnut wood wand is suitable for a beginner due to its gentle and docile energy. She will bring abundance of the mind to her wonder.

And the yew tree, my long-standing friend. Every part of the yew is highly poisonous, including the bark, berries, and seeds. It carries this energy through its wood, providing us with properties of protection and banishment. Yew is wonderful for ancestor connection. She is centered around the cycle of life and supports the eternal renewal of the soul.

# Seasons of the woods

## BIRCH TREE

*December 24 to January 20*

## ROWAN TREE

*January 21 to February 11*

## ASH TREE

*February 18 to March 17*

## ALDER TREE

*March 18 to April 14*

## WILLOW TREE

*April 15 to May 12*

## HAWTHORN TREE

*May 13 to June 9*

## OAK TREE

*June 10 to July 7*

## HOLLY TREE

*July 8 to August 4*

## HAZEL TREE

*August 5 to September 1*

## VINE

*September 2 to September 29*

## IVY

*September 30 to October 27*

## REED

*October 28 to November 23*

## ELDER TREE

*November 24 to December 23*

> *Dirt from the garden of your home has a highly stabilizing and grounding energy.*

## DIRTS AND DUSTS

Dirt contains the spiritual essence of the earth, or if gathered around a particular plant or tree, the properties of that root. It can be used for a multitude of things: Guarding the home, applying to bug bites, healing the soul, for example. I use a variety of dirts in my practice, as follows:

### Garden dirt

Dirt from the garden of your home has a highly stabilizing and grounding energy. Use this type of dirt in spells to heal the family and home, specifically centering around protection and abundance. You can also use it in spells to protect your family, and should carry some on your person to keep that protection with you. Dirt from your garden has an especially stable energy and can be used to encourage things to grow.

### Bank dirt

Dirt from a bank is useful in spells dealing with money, finances, and business ventures. When you are dealing with spiritual transactions, dirt from a bank is an especially powerful ingredient. There are other items from a bank that can be used for a similar purpose, such as deposit slips, dust, or receipts.

### Legal dirt

Dirt or dust from a courthouse can be used in spells for positive outcomes in legal matters and court cases, or more generally for any spell related to getting justice. Legal dirt is especially lucky, and can be used to increase gambling odds.

### Crossroads dirt

Dirt from a crossroads (a place where two or more roads intersect, forming a cross) is especially useful for working with spirits, as crossroads are believed to be one of the liminal places where souls can more easily cross over. Some traditions use crossroads dirt as an all-round power boost for any type of spell. It is also used specifically to remove obstacles and open up opportunities.

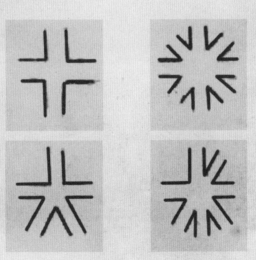

# SHELLS

The sensual snail has long been held to be a creature of fertile, potent, and blessed virtue. Most fortunate of all is a distinctly striped snail shell, which, upon discovery, is to be immediately pocketed as a personal lucky charm. Despite their small size, snail shells bring a powerful spirit to magical work due to the nature of the shell itself. A snail's shell is always connected to death, as a snail cannot live without its shell. When we find these shells, it means that the snails that inhabited them have died, usually because they've been eaten by birds or insects. This is an important point to keep in mind, not just as we work with the spirit of the snail and the snail shell, but as we collect them. While it can be exciting to find a large collection of snail shells for our work, we should remember that each one represents a life—however small it may be.

There are many types of shells around the world: Sea shells, crustacean shells, for example. However, snail have unique properties. They are as protective as they are fertile, carrying the defensive properties that the shell provided for the snail. They can also be carried as a defensive amulet or, if they are small enough, placed in a bottle. To process snail shells for use in powder, use a hammer or mallet to break them into pieces and then use a mortar and pestle to grind them up further into a fine powder. Sprinkle this powder when prosperity or protection is needed.

A reliable way to increase abundance around the home is to gather shells from a lakeshore and string them up in clusters around the house. Another alternative is to crush these shells and scatter them across the doorstep on the first day of the month.

# WATER

In the same way that there are different types of dirt, so too are there numerous kinds of water that possess the characteristics of where that water resides. Water can greatly aid in any magical workings, as it is a natural amplifier of the aquatic elements. Below are my preferred types of water to use:

## Well water

Well water is typically calm, clear water that springs up from the earth. It is most often used for healing and purification as well as for astral travel and connecting with the other side. The smooth surface is perfect for scrying and water divination. It can also be used for removing curses as well as placing them.

## Stump water

This is water that naturally collects in a tree stump or hole in a tree. Stump water is considered to have healing properties beyond measure. It's also considered lucky. Charms, such as a rabbit's foot, can be dipped in stump water to enhance its lucky properties. Furthermore, stump water is stagnated water, making it perfect for scrying, ancestral work, spirit communication, or as a portal. The water also takes on the property of the tree in which it is found and can, therefore, be used to mimic the tree's power in spellwork.

## Swamp water

Swamp water is often dirty, filled with decaying plant matter. In some cases, the water is also stagnant. Marsh water can be used in hexes and curses, to stagnate a situation, to cover or hide something, and even during ancestral work. Swamp water is often associated with death and decay, making it the perfect water to use when working with the dead.

## Lake water

As lake water is often calm and mirror-like, it can be used in divination work such as scrying. It is also useful in healing spells and rituals, as well as cleansing, purification, relaxation, or revitalizing spells. On the other hand, lake water gathered from a particularly gusty November storm is the perfect way to create chaos in spellwork.

# MUSHROOMS

Invocation is the action that sets the spellwork into motion. By adding a physicality to our spells, we are signaling to the universe that we are ready for action. Mushrooms are an ingredient that promises immediate action when used, similar to a strong invocation, as they are a symbol of fast growth and expansion. There are a number of folk magic uses for mushrooms, and you can incorporate these at a symbolic level, rather than actually ingesting them.

To gather mushrooms you should use a woven basket; the spores of the mushrooms will be free to fall out of the basket once gathered, thus sowing a new harvest. Foraging and identifying mushrooms is not an easy task, as there are many imposters for most species. If you are in any way unsure of what kind of mushroom it is, DO NOT consume it. Contact a local mushroom expert who may be able to help you learn to identify mushrooms safely. Handling, eating, and interacting with mushrooms is a sacred and potentially perilous task, and should be treated as such. Here are some of the most common mushrooms to use in the region of the north:

## Bolete

The species of bolete mushrooms run far and wide; however, they are all used for their characteristics of strength, similar to the oak. Use boletes in spellwork as an intensifying agent. Boletes that grow in clusters can be used in family or household workings.

## Chanterelle

These mushrooms are commonly found under hardwood trees. However, they can also be foraged under pine and fir. If you find a patch of these mushrooms, sit in it. Simply being in the presence of chanterelles is enough to bring success to the lone friend of these mushrooms. Gifting a chanterelle to a person you desire a relationship with is a good way to kindle the fire.

## Lion's mane

The lion's mane best represents fertility and is famously known for bringing good luck. Even spotting a mane is said to bless the seeker with good fortune. This mushroom can be dried and placed on an altar to attract growth and abundance. When used as an offering, it is said to attract loving spirits.

*Invocation is the action that sets the spellwork into motion.*

## Hen of the woods

Similar to most mushrooms, the hen of the woods offers ways to increase fertility and fruitfulness for whatever endeavor you choose. Hen of the woods carries great strength in the area of rebirth, allowing for us to turn over a new leaf when we feel stuck. The cycle of the mushrooms is symbolic, showing us how quickly we can grow and change. Following the ways of the mushroom, or using the hen of the woods in spellwork, is a perfect way to invoke change.

## Ink cap

These fungi get their names from the Latin word *atramentum*, meaning ink. This perfectly symbolizes how the ink cap has been used for centuries—as ink, espeifically to prevent forgery in important documents, since the spores of the mushrooms can be detected in the ink. That being said, ink caps might be my favorite mushroom to use in protective wards, as they are said to conceal the user from whatever they desire. It is particularly useful for having magic go undetected in secretive workings. This Plutonian plant represents confidentiality, giving us an ingredient to utilize whenever we need to go into hiding.

## Morel

The morel is the giver of knowledge, as it often represents the brain or nervous system. They hold the secrets of the seasons and decide when spring passes into summer. It is said that if you can actually find the morel, you can gain a fraction of its knowledge. It often feels as if you are discovering a secret. The morel doesn't mind, as he is happy to share his wisdom.

## Oyster

The oyster mushroom is a famed aphrodisiac, helpful in increasing love and lust. Growing in large groups on the sides of trees, they are ideal for bringing a community together and inciting new friendships. Emotional healing is the oyster mushroom's strong suit, as well as forgiveness of others and the self.

# STONES

Stones are studied in a unique way and unforgiving in their energy. They stand tall in their ways, waiting for you to tap into the mysteries of their energy. Many different types of crystals, stones, and minerals can be found all around the world. However, I've always felt most drawn to those found on the lakeshore of my small town.

Stones can be powerhouses of energy, acting as a conduit for bringing our intention into the universe. To understand the magic behind stones, we have to understand their birthplace. They are formed deep within the earth and hold its potent energy. Similar to herbs, each stone has its own metaphysical properties due to its formation, makeup, and other mineral attributes.

The one thing I've found most compelling about my work with crystals is the fact that the stone will never change. My mom always told me "a stone is more likely to change you than you are likely to change a stone." They are simply a tool that already possesses its designated energy, and that energy will not waver no matter how often you use it. I find it important to align your intention with the properties of the stone to fully alchemize its use.

The stones of Northern Michigan are unique to this area, covering the beaches far and wide. While the rocks come in a rainbow assortment of colors, sizes, and mineral properties, I experience a particular connection to five types of stones, as follows.

## Hagstones

I was always taught that hagstones are lucky. As children, we used to search the shore for stones and shells with holes in them to make mobiles, necklaces, or charms. Hagstones are stones that have a hole running all the way through them, and are usually found in streams, rivers, and along the seashore where running water has created the hole in the stone. They're often found on the beach or by waterfalls, both considered to be liminal places and therefore magical in themselves.

This may be one of the reasons why they are considered so powerful, as these stones have been bored out by running water and so retain that energy. It's all in the hole, you see. The theory goes that only good things can pass through a hole, so while good fortune and good wishes will find you through a hagstone, bad luck and evil thoughts are too big to to pass through the hole and become stuck in the middle.

As wish stones, hagstones are held in the palm of the left hand and rubbed with the thumb in a clockwise direction while repeating the intent of the wish—specifically in threes, as explained below. Threading a cord through the hole and wearing the hagstone around your neck will give you protection. You can also protect your house by hanging hagstones in the doorways and windows. Stones with multiple holes are used as spell-casting stones. A cord or pebble can be passed through the holes in patterns of three, while the intent of the spell is repeated, usually in multiples of three. Livestock owners can use the stones to protect their animals from danger. In the past, a stone would be suspended by a cord in the center of each stable to protect the horses and other livestock. It was even said to prevent the farmers' cows from giving sour milk, or hens from refusing to lay eggs. Fishermen and sailors would tie the stones found on beaches to their boats to ward off evil spirits and sirens from affecting their vessels and their catch.

## Lake Superior agates

Lake Superior agates, or lakers, are a type of agate that is found in the Midwestern area. These unique stones formed during lava eruptions in the Great Lakes and are famously stained red by the presence of iron deposits. I grew up longing to find a laker, only to discover my first one at the age of sixteen. Over the last few years, I've come to gather a collection of 12 lakers.

Each one holds its unique characteristics: Banding of oranges and yellows, craters and holes both big and small. And, over time, they have grown to be my favorite type of crystal or stone. While I only possess a few, their power is immeasurable. Finding one on the shoreline give me a similar feeling to striking gold.

Because they were formed during a period of change, these agates are especially helpful in guiding us through challenging periods of adaptation. It is an especially grounding stone, allowing me to feel pulled to the core of nature and the center of spiritual comfort. Look inside my pockets any day, and you will find that I'm carrying a laker. I often find myself rhythmically rubbing the stone in circles when I'm anxious, which helps to center my breathing and bringing me back to reality.

Another method of using a laker is to place it under your pillow to ward off nightmares. As a stone of adaptability and flexibility, it helps us find the

> Fishermen and sailors would tie the stones found on beaches to their boats to ward off evil spirits and sirens ...

strength to make it through a rough dream. One can be worn as a protection amulet, used to draw in the natural defensive powers of Mother Nature.

## Petoskey stones

Petoskey stones are the most sought-after stone of the Northern Michigan area. Tourists arrive from far and wide to walk the beaches in search of this mysterious stone. These unique fossils are a result of formations of coral that once lived within the Great Lakes. I've found through my years of rock hunting that the fall season is the best for finding Petoskey stones. The waves from the November gales push the rocks onto the shore, revealing stones that haven't seen the surface of the lakes in years.

Lake Michigan beaches are typically the most common place to find Petoskey stones, but they are also found in the oddest of locations—gravel pits, roadbeds, driveways, rivers, and even fields. They can be difficult to spot when they are dry, appearing as a plain gray limestone. Get a Petoskey stone wet and it will quickly reveal the hexagonal patterns of the fossilized coral.

It is said that the hexagonal patterns, similar to the shape of an eye, can enhance psychic perception. Petoskey stones are naturally intuitional, helping in knowing our own emotions and influencing our expression. When I hold a Petoskey stone, I feel the deep information it holds, awakening the senses and preparing the brain to receive messages intuitively.

While the spiritually enhancing properties of the stones are very strong, allowing us to connect with our innermost desires, they can also work to balance or even reduce psychic visions or messages from the spirit, etc. It is both grounding and spiritually enticing, raising our awareness and revitalizing our soul when needed. The Petoskey stone will help you if you're having trouble controlling your channeling abilities.

*Often known as the master healer, quartz is notorious for its adaptability and ever-changing qualities.*

I've discovered that the Petoskey stone is most effective worn in the form of an amulet. Crafters all around Northern Michigan provide beautiful handmade Petoskey stone jewelry, which I personally wear when engaging in divination or spirit work.

## Quartz

Quartz found on the shores of Lake Michigan can range from clear to smoky as well as orange, red, yellow, and white. Although many struggle to find these little gems, they litter the beaches far and wide. Never underestimate the power of a pebble of quartz, as it is often known to be an amplifier hidden among the rest.

Often known as the master healer, quartz is notorious for its adaptability and ever-changing qualities. Whatever intention you put into a piece of quartz, it is known to fall out tenfold. It is also thought to be able to amplify, decrease, or balance any situation, depending on your intent. Quartz is a versatile stone, found throughout the world. However, the quartz that is only found in the Great Lakes carries the energy of the water throughout the grains of the stone.

I think of each piece of quartz found on the beach as a droplet of water from the lake herself. Taking a single stone is enough to capture her abilities. A piece of her quartz can be used to invoke change in your life. Carry a piece of quartz found on the Great Lakes for a quick change of direction. Using this type of quartz in a spell is a powerful way to influence the strings of fate.

## Wishing stones

Local lore says that if you find a stone with a full line around the circumference, you have found a wishing stone. A wishing stone can be of any type, as long as there's a line around it. This band can be of any thickness, but there should only be one and it should be unbroken. Large or small, red or black, wishing stones come in a variety of shapes, sizes, and colors. The very best wishing stone is dark in color, with a single continuous line wrapped around it, uninterrupted by other lines or streaks.

The way I was taught to use a wishing stone is to trace your finger around the line while closing your eyes and making a wish before throwing the stone into the lake as far as you can. Then your wish will come true. Another magical use for the wishing stone is to make a wish about a lover, and then give it to the object of your desires. A wishing stone can also be carried on the body daily to increase general luck and prosperity.

*It is said that the hexagonal patterns can enhance psychic perception.*

# CHAPTER EIGHT

# Spellcraft

## SPELLWORK

### Lunar correspondence

### Spell formulation

### The working space

### The spells

# Spellwork

SPELLWORK AND HEALING RITES CAN BE PERFORMED BY JUST ABOUT ANYONE. HOWEVER, THERE ARE A FEW DIFFERENT SIGNS THAT MIGHT SHOW THAT A PERSON HAS THE GIFT FOR HEALING OR SPELLCRAFT. MANY OF THESE SIGNS CAN BE SEEN FROM BIRTH. CHILDREN BORN ON THE BRINK OF DEATH OFTEN POSSESS HEALING ABILITIES PRESENT SINCE BIRTH. GENERALLY SPEAKING, ANY ODD COLORATION OR MARKINGS AT BIRTH CAN POINT TOWARD BEING A CARRIER OF THE GIFT.

Surviving a serious disease or injury can also mark a person out to receive the gift. Folks who have had near-death experiences often begin to show signs that they did not exhibit before. A baby born at or near to the death of another family member is said to receive the gift from this crossing of the two worlds. I've even heard of mothers passing their gifts to their children if they pass in childbirth. If a person acquires their gift through such means, they are called a seer.

Often the gift comes to a person with no signs at all, which is simply referred to as knowing. They sometimes just seem to have an innate ability to do things, as they say, or to pick up and learn skills from others. While the gift runs in my family, I showed no obvious signs of it. My brother, on the other hand, passed to the other side when he was born. He spent year after year in the hospitals with an incurable ailment of seemingly dying and coming back to life.

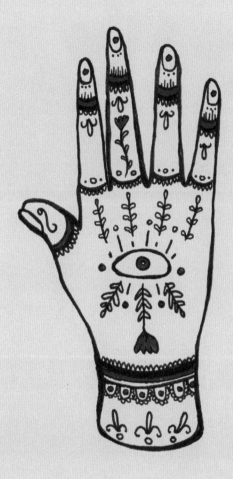

This, of course, rendered him very susceptible to receiving the gift. Just because somebody is called a "knower" or a "seer" does not mean that their abilities are secret and exclusive to those with the gift. It just means these abilities come more easily to them, often without previous knowledge or instructions. These skills can be taught and transferred to whoever the teacher sees fit. All it takes is a ready mind and a will to continue even in the toughest of times. Even with the gift of "knowing," the more I think I know, the more I discover there is to learn. We can all benefit from learning from those around us, and the greatest of teachers lay in plain sight. My mom has taught me some of the best spells and remedies that she learned from her mom, who learned it from her mom. Most of these techniques are ingrained into our daily existence, so much so that it has become a way of life.

We use the moon, the stars, and the faint planets when they solemnly choose to show us when to sow the seeds of life. The planets speak quietly, the stars show us what we need to see, but the moon is always there.

# LUNAR CORRESPONDENCE

The old folk have long had faith in the ability of the moon to impart virtue, blessing, and fecundity. There are well-kept small and simple rites surrounding the moon, observed in order to ensure good fortune, and its preservation.

Each stage has a different part to play in the work being done. A waxing moon is always used for when you want something to grow. Take, for instance, making a good luck charm when the moon is waxing—as the moon grows, so too will your luck. Likewise, a waning moon is for whenever you want something to diminish or rot away.

To be more specific, the new moon is when the sun and the moon are on the same side of the earth. The new moon not only represents a fresh start but also a time of retreat—a time when you can regain your strength to start over. The spiritual themes surrounding the new moon are new beginnings, fresh starts, and clean slates.

Some use this as a time of contemplation and self-reflection, but this can also be done in later moon phases. The new moon is, as its name suggests, a good time to do any kind of spell, because there's a new energy in the world. When the moon is hidden, it can be useful to focus on the hidden parts of your life, or things that you want to bring to the surface.

The waxing crescent is the official moon phase for setting intentions. This can also be used as a time to act on your intentions. This phase represents intention, hopes, and wishes, and it is the time when you should begin to develop your desires for the month ahead by laying down the mental groundwork.

It is the best time to perform spells for growth, beginning new projects, initiation, and enhancement. "Increase" is the operative word, just as the moon is increasing. The energy of the waxing crescent is all about determining what you want more of before you start thinking about and envisioning what you want to bring forth from the external world.

The first quarter is the phase for starting to act on our intentions. This is challenging as typically we start noticing obstacles and hurdles to our goals. It's important to make decisions and create action plans that allow us to push through and jump over the obstacles. When the first quarter is occurring, it's the perfect time to acknowledge what your deepest wishes are. This is also a time to figure out what is in your way.

The quarter moon is all about attraction from the external world. It's the optimal time for performing magic that aims to draw things in, whether it's a person, success, or money. This is also a very conducive time to call back lost objects.

The waxing gibbous is a time to further refine your intention and fine-tune it into exactly what you want—revisit your new moon and crescent work to do this accurately. We must put in the final push of effort as we are heading to full moon energy; this is the last bit of effort we need to use waxing energy to move things forward. Add to what you have been working with.

Still in the constructive magic phase, the energies of the waxing gibbous moon are great for giving that extra energy to something you've been working on but which may have been stagnating.

Full moons are a time of collecting our manifesting, sealing intentions, and release. Let go of your expectations and allow the universe simply to make it happen. The full moon is renowned as the most popular phase, showing the moon in its full glory. Its intensity is often saved for some of our most powerful spells and intentions. This is a prime time for rituals for prophecy, protection, and divination. Any work that needs extra power, such as help finding a new job or healing for serious conditions, can be done now.

Under the waning gibbous is where you want to be releasing the ideas, patterns, behaviors, situations, and even people who are no longer serving your highest good. In some ways, the waning moon phase is when we are really focused on our inward needs and innermost thoughts and feelings.

Use this phase to perform spells and rituals aimed at minor banishings and cleansings, whether in physical terms or bringing closure mentally. Here, "decrease" is the operative word, as the moon's light is now decreasing.

The last quarter signifies forgiveness. Remember that forgiveness isn't for the person in question to feel better—it's only for you. You do not have to forgive someone if you feel they do not deserve it. Last quarter rituals can be powerful catalysts for healing and letting go of negative energy that can stagnate and hang around if we aren't mindful.

The waning crescent phase is about surrendering. Hold gratitude in your heart and release what doesn't serve you as you move into the darkness of the new moon. This is also a great time to reflect on yourself.

As we get closer to the new moon phase, energies are more suitable for performing bigger banishings, such as getting rid of anything that has been absorbing joy from your life and draining your energy.

Work for healing sickness and performing charms is almost always done during the waning moon. The new moon is for adding a little extra power to anything new that you're starting, while the full moon is for coming to fruition. The new moon is also especially useful for dream divination and working with the spirit world.

*There are well-kept rites surrounding the moon*

# SPELL FORMULATION

The techniques involved in spellwork are inconspicuous to the outside viewer, never giving away our intent. We choose to make what we do into a magical work, because that's the only way the old folks could avoid persecution. The making of a spell can include a candle-burning ceremony, making a witch's bottle, or simply just knitting.

However modest these incantations and workings may seem, there is quite a lot of formulation going on behind the scenes. The anatomy of a spell is crucial to understanding the ways in which a spell manifests itself into reality.

Intent and Will are two parts of the "formula" for effective spellcraft. The "formula" has a lot of permutations, and is not always adhered to, but is essentially as follows:

## Intent + Will + Action = Spell

**INTENT** *is the statement behind your spell, whether it be mental, verbal, or physical. For instance, if you're working for a better memory, "having a better memory" is your intent.*

**WILL** *is the energy that fuels your spell through your personal decisions and action. Will is what you personally do to make your spell work.*

**ACTION** *is the word I use for the physicality of the spell or ritual, the actual actions performed. For example, burning a candle, shaking a jar, a spoken invocation, etc ...*

*Now, there are many different types of workings and spells: Protections, pullings, purifications, etc. However, they will generally include these three elements. The technicalities behind each type of working is intricate, and ultimately, up to the worker.*

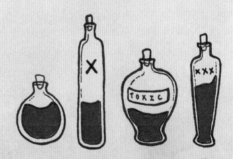

> *I work everywhere, from the kitchen table to the stump out in the backyard, and take my tools as I go.*

## THE WORKING SPACE

The ancestor altar is used for purposes of communication, veneration, and maybe divination; the working altar is quite often simple—a table that you can frequently turn to, or a countertop empty and ready to use in preparations and rites. Nothing is really needed for a working space except the tools you feel connected to and you, yourself, ready to work. This altar does not have to be permanent, and it can grow as you do.

I work everywhere, from the kitchen table to the stump out in the backyard, and take my tools as I go.

To me, a working altar is not much more than a space that aids me in what I need to get done. Everybody's workspace looks fitted to their craft. However, I often like to keep the following items nearby: An athame or knife, a cast-iron cauldron, a hagstone, and a handkerchief. The athame is useful for many purposes—slicing, dividing, poking, for example. A cauldron can be used to cook and boil. A hagstone kept nearby is enough to protect your working space for the time being, and the handkerchief catches the blood and sweat of hard work.

## THE SPELLS

Here is my attempt to organize a cohesive list of the hectic spellwork I've learned throughout the years. The following are my absolute favorite workings and folk remedies for everything from luck to cleansing the home. Remember to take precautions when doing any type of work, employing spirits, etc. ... and be aware of the self, as we are the source of energy in all workings.

## Removal of troubling energy

***Ingredients*: 1 Egg**

1  Pass the egg over every area of your or another person's body.

2  Once the egg has absorbed anything that might be troubling you or the other person, destroy the egg far from the home by throwing it in a river or smashing it against a tree.

# To make a wish come true

*Ingredients: Apple, Piece of Paper, Red String, Red Candle*

**1** Cut an apple in half from top to bottom.

**2** Then, gather a pen and paper. Write a note of who or what you desire on this piece of paper.

**3** Place the paper between the two apple halves.

**4** Secure the apple back together with a red ribbon or string.

**5** Seal the edges of the cut apple with a red candle.

**6** Bury under your front door once the apple has rotted.

# Healing others from afar

**Ingredients: Ginger Root, Plant Pot,
1 Hagstone**

1  Plant the ginger root in a sturdy pot.

2  Place the pot on a windowsill or somewhere sunny facing in
   the direction of where your loved one lives.

3  Place a hagstone in the dirt over the ginger root. As it sprouts
   through the hagstone, tend to it daily to ensure its growth.

# cleansing bath

*Ingredients: Skullcap, Calendula, Juniper*

1 Run a steaming hot bath whenever you feel a buildup of negative energy inside you or in your surrounding area.

2 Sprinkle in equal amount of skullcap, calendula, and juniper into the bathtub once filled with water.

3 Soak in the bath for around ten minutes; enough time to wash away your troubles, but never soak for too long.

# Snail shell safety spell

**Ingredients: 1 Snail Shell, Dirt from your Front Yard,
Rosemary, Hydrangea, Black Candle**

1 Fill half the snail shell with dirt from your
front yard.

2 Add rosemary to the shell.

3 Add hydrangea last.

4 Seal the opening of the shell with the wax from
a black candle.

5 Once you have a sealed shell, hide it under your stairs or
above a doorway and never move it.

# A sachet for luck

*Ingredients: Dirt from the Garden, Burlap Bag, Queen Anne's Lace Root, Rabbit's Foot, A Striped Snail Shell, Ribbon or String*

1  On a waxing gibbous moon, gather dirt from your front or backyard and pour it into a burlap bag.

2  Add the Queen Anne's lace root, a rabbit's foot, and a striped snail shell to the bag.

3  Close the bag and tie it shut with a length of ribbon or string.

4  Shake the bag vigorously whenever luck is needed.

5  The bag can also be carried daily in order to increase general prosperity.

# To find a lost object

### *Ingredients: 1 Iron Nail*

1  Place a nail on a windowsill.

2  Blow on the nail to make it spin.

3  The nail should point you in the direction of wherever your lost item lies.

4  When you have located the object, bury or hide the nail where you found it.

5  Repeat when needed.

# A change of fate

*Ingredients: Red String, Black Candle,*
*White Candle, Bay Leaf*

1 On a new moon, gather a red string and two candles; one will represent the past and one will represent the future.

2 Tie the candles together with the red string, leaving a considerable amount of string between them.

3 Write your manifestation on a bay leaf.

4 Ignite both candles with the flame of the burning bay leaf.

5 Observe how the candles burn and melt.

6 Take note of any particular objects, symbols, and suchlike you see in the wax, as these can provide insight on the future you want to influence.

# Ridding yourself of worries

### Ingredients: Twine, Rope, or String

1  To rid yourself of worries, tie knots in a piece of twine, rope, or string for each troublesome thought you have.

2  Repeat these thoughts aloud as you tie knots along the rope.

3  Bury the rope in your backyard and never dig it up.

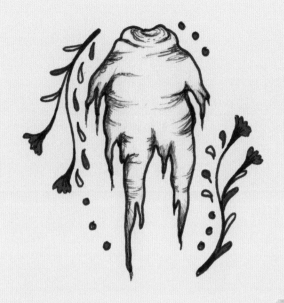

# Binding yourself to success

*Ingredients: 1 Solomon's Seal Root,*
*Bundles of Basil, Green String*

1 Take a Solomon's seal root that resembles the shape of a person.

2 Gather two bundles of basil and bind them to each side of the root with a piece of green string.

3 Bury the root under your front doorstep on a waxing crescent moon to ensure success within the next moon cycle.

# 4

## Money bowl for wealth

*Ingredients: Banknote, Green Bowl, Dirt or other item from a bank, Salt, Bay Leaves, Silver Coins, Mirror*

1 On a Thursday, write your desired intention onto the banknote and place it under the green bowl.

2 Add the dirt or other item from a bank to build a stable foundation.

3 Add salt to protect your money.

4 Write your lucky number on the bay leaf and add it to the bowl.

5 Place the silver coins around the perimeter of the bowl.

6 Place the bowl in front of the mirror.

7 As your pockets grow fuller, add a part of your earnings to the bowl and never spend it.

# Protection from the evil eye

**Ingredients: Red Woolen String**

1  To ward off the evil eye, a red woolen string is often tied in seven knots around the wrist.

2  When the string is torn or lost, it has completed its purpose or protection of the wearer.

3  This broken string is no longer of use—so a new one should be tied.

# Protection from spirits

### Ingredients: 10 Almonds

**1** Begin every day with 10 almonds in your left pocket to
protect you from spirits.

**2** Before you enter your doorway, eat the remaining
almonds in your pocket.

**3** It's okay to lose some—it means they did their job.

# Seeking romantic resolutions

*Ingredients: Picture of You,*
*Picture of your Subject,*
*Rose Petals*

1 If you want to find resolution between you and your partner, look for a picture of each of you.

2 Place the two pictures face to face.

3 Stick a rose petal between the two pictures.

4 Place the pictures in your underwear drawer on a waxing moon until a resolution has been reached.

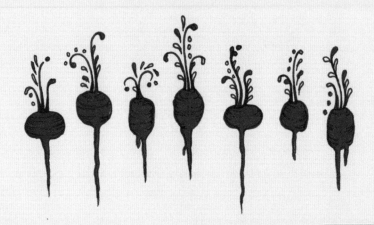

# Protection of the house

*Ingredients: 7 Turnips, Shovel*

1  To protect your house from spirits, ill wishes, and other
   negativity, bury seven turnips under your front step where
   you will walk over them every day.

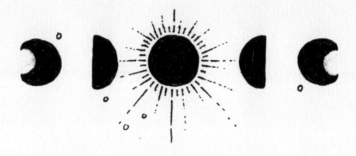

# Making money under the moon

*Ingredients: Coins, Jar*

1 Starting on the new moon and continuing throughout the month, collect your coins into a large jar.

2 Once the full moon comes, stand outside and shake your jar of money at the moon.

3 Continue adding to your jar and shake it during every full moon.

## Shake your jar of money at the moon.

# Oil to return energy to its sender

*Ingredients: Yarrow, Mullein, Dropper Bottle, Amaranth Oil, Red String*

1 On a waning crescent moon, gather your ingredients.

2 Add yarrow and mullein to the dropper bottle.

3 Fill the dropper bottle with the amaranth oil.

4 Wrap the red string around the neck of the bottle many, many times.

5 Each time you use the oil, unwrap a bit of the string.

6 This oil can be used on the skin, in spells, to anoint candles, and much, much more.

# cleansing the house of energy

***Ingredients: Cauldron, Juniper,***
***Mint, Rosemary, Small Cauldron***

1  Open a window in your house to allow the negative energy to escape.

2  Add one sprig each of juniper, mint, and rosemary into your cauldron.

3  Burn the contents of the cauldron as you walk through each room of your house.

# Growing self-love

### *Ingredients: Blackberry Leaves, Fennel, Forget-Me-Not Flowers, Ginger, Jar, Mirror*

**1**  Add all four plant ingredients to the jar.

**2**  Once the jar is full, speak loving words of encouragement into the jar.

**3**  Quickly close the lid.

**4**  Place this jar near a mirror.

**5**  Reopen and speak into the jar when needed.

# Protection for a sibling

*Ingredients: Black Candle, Amaranth Oil,*
*Dried Mulberry Leaves, Mortar and Pestle,*
*7 Rose Thorns*

1 Anoint the black candle with amaranth oil.

2 Grind the mulberry leaves into a fine powder.

3 Roll the anointed candle in the mulberry leaf powder.

4 Impale the candle with seven rose thorns.

5 Burn the candle whenever you feel protection is needed for your sibling.

# For safe travels

*Ingredients: Comfrey, Ferns, Leek, Small Jar, Hagstone, Fox Foot Bone, Purple Thread or String, Black Candle*

**1** Add in comfrey, ferns, and a leek into a small jar.

**2** Bind the hagstone and the fox foot bone together with purple thread or string.

**3** Add in the bound hagstone and foot bone to the jar.

**4** Seal the jar with wax from a black candle.

**5** Carry this jar with you or place it in your car to invoke a feeling of safety.

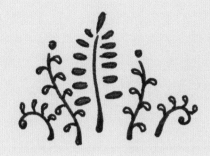

# To banish nightmares

*Ingredients: Red Flannel Bag, Juniper,*
*Yarrow, Rue, Thread or String*

1  Sleep with the red flannel bag under your pillow for five
   nights before starting this spell.

2  After five days, add in juniper, yarrow, and rue to the bag.

3  Close the bag and tie it tightly with thread or string.

4  Place the filled bag back under your pillow to help protect
   you against nightmares.

# Sleep with the red flannel bag under your pillow.

# Oil for ancestor communication

*Ingredients: Mugwort, Lavender, Dropper Bottle, Rosehip Oil, Ghost Pipes*

1 On a full moon, gather together your ingredients.

2 Add mugwort and lavender to the dropper bottle.

3 Fill the dropper bottle with the rosehip oil.

4 Add a pinch of crushed ghost pipe to the top of the dropper bottle.

5 Shake the oil to combine the ingredients.

6 This oil can be used on the skin, in spells, to anoint candles, and more to enhance our connection with the divine.

# Making new friends

*Ingredients: Piece of Paper, Envelope, Sweet Pea Flowers,
Rosehips, Lemongrass, Joe Pye Weed*

**1** Write on a piece of paper how you would like to pursue a friendship
with your subject and the reason why.

**2** Fold the paper three times toward you and place it into the envelope.

**3** Sprinkle sweet pea flowers, rosehips, lemongrass, and a pinch of
Joe Pye weed into the envelope.

**4** Seal the envelope and keep it safe until your wish manifests into reality.

# Disappearing from the public eye

*Ingredients: Rue, Fern, Fennel,
Jar, Mortar and Pestle*

**1** Dry each ingredient so it can be easily crushed and ground up.

**2** Add the dried rue, fern, and fennel to your mortar and grind it into a fine powder.

**3** Store this powder in a jar.

**4** Sprinkle the powder over your head when you are looking for some solitude.

# Spellcrafting notes

_____
_____
_____
_____
_____
_____
_____
_____
_____
_____
_____
_____
_____
_____
_____
_____
_____
_____

# Spellcrafting notes

_____

_____

_____

_____

_____

_____

_____

_____

_____

_____

_____

_____

_____

_____

_____

_____

_____

# Spellcrafting notes

_____

_____

_____

_____

_____

_____

_____

_____

_____

_____

_____

_____

_____

_____

# Index

**Author's website**
Find out more about Kiley and buy witchcraft supplies at kileymannart.com.